Extended RV Travel

How To Travel In Your RV
For Weeks Or Months At A Time

by Joe and Vicki Kieva

Extended RV Travel

Copyright © 1998 by Joe and Vicki Kieva

All rights reserved. No part of this book may be reproduced, stored or transmitted in any form or by any mechanical or electronic means without prior written permission from the publisher.

First Printing 1998
Second Printing 2001, Revised

ISBN # 0-9655620-2-6

Published by RV Travel Adventures
P.O. Box 5055
Huntington Beach, CA 92615

www.rvknowhow.com

Printed in the United States of America

Contents

Start RVing Now	1
Home Security And Maintenance	7
Banking And Bill Paying	11
Receiving Mail	16
Medical Care And Prescriptions	18
Telephone Communications	22
Computers and RVs	27
E-mail On The Road	31
Choosing An RV For Extended Travel	34
Slideout Rooms	43
Switching From Gas To Diesel	48
Choosing A Tow Vehicle	58
Dinghy Towing	61
Microwave/Convection Ovens	65
Clothes Washer/Dryers	67
What To Take	69
Selecting Campgrounds	74
Locating Uncrowded Campgrounds	79
Self-Contained Camping	81
Cold-Weather Camping	86
RVing On A Budget	92
Fuel Expenses	95
Membership Campgrounds	98
Safety and Security	102
Traveling With Pets	108
RV Travel Tips	111
Making Money On The Road	114
Missing The Grandchildren	122
Familiar Places	125
Information To Go	127

About The Authors

RV travel adventurers, Joe and Vicki Kieva, have over 35 years of RVing experience. Their extensive travels, in a variety of RVs, have taken them throughout the United States, Canada and Mexico.

Joe and Vicki have escorted RV caravans to Mexico and Alaska, taught RV classes at community colleges around the country and authored two other books, *RVing Made Easy* and *RVing Tips, Tricks And Techniques*. Their "how-to" RV advice columns appear monthly in a number of regional and national RV magazines.

Since 1993 they have been sharing their knowledge and experience by touring the country in their RV and presenting seminars at RV shows, rallies and other special events.

Between RV trips Joe and Vicki reside in a house near their children and grandchildren in Huntington Beach, California

Introduction

In 1974 we made a dream come true. We left our jobs; pulled three kids out of school; loaded up a 17-foot travel trailer and began a five-month tour of North America.

We camped in national parks, toured the Smithsonian Institute and visited an endless number of tourist attractions.

We came home thoroughly addicted to extended RV travel. Never again would a two or three-week vacation satisfy our wanderlust. We changed our lifestyle to accommodate at least one six-to-eight week trip every year.

In 1989 we made another dream come true. We left our jobs so we could devote even more time to RV travel.

Today we spend two to three months at a time on the road. Between trips we return to our house in California. It only takes a month or two, though, before wanderlust gets the best of us and we are on the road again.

During our travels we present seminars at RV shows, rallies and other events. We also write for RV magazines.

Judging by the questions we get from those who attend our seminars and read our columns, there are a lot of RVers who are interested in becoming extended travelers.

This book is an attempt to answer the questions most frequently asked about extended RV travel.

We hope this book will help you make your dreams come true. Be careful, though, you too may succumb to the lure of the open road and find yourself addicted to the joys of extended RV travel.

Enjoy The Journey!

Extended - stretched out, continued or prolonged.

RV - vehicle providing mobile living accommodations.

Traveler - one who goes from place to place.

Extended RV Traveler - one who goes from place to place in an RV for prolonged periods of time.

Start RVing Now

"I'm retiring in four years and when I do, I'm going to sell my house, buy an RV and be a full-time RVer."

Joe: We hear that dream expressed all the time. Unfortunately, the dreamer is often a person who has no RVing experience whatsoever. He doesn't know anything about the lifestyle he is planning to enter. He just hopes it will be an escape from the way of life he has built for himself over the last 30 or 40 years.

Now, don't get me wrong. A good number of people with no RVing background have retired or quit their jobs and successfully joined the ranks of those who live and travel full time in their RVs. Some have even written educational and entertaining books about their experiences.

We haven't seen many books, though, by those whose dreams were shattered because they bought the wrong RV or by those who spent a lot of money just to learn they were not cut out for RVing. And how many people have sold their home only to discover that while they enjoy traveling in an RV they prefer living in a house?

Vicki: Here's what we suggest to those who are looking forward to an RVing retirement. Don't wait until you retire. Start now to prepare for the lifestyle you are dreaming about. Buy an RV today. Start RVing now. Use the years before your retirement to learn about RVs, RVing and yourself.

You may discover that you don't want to sell your house and be a fulltimer. You may decide, instead, that extended RV travel is what you prefer to do. You might even learn that RVing is not how you want to spend your retirement after all.

The best way to learn is through experience. So start now. Buy an RV. It doesn't have to be new or expensive. Think of it as a training rig. This is the one you will use as a benchmark when you go out to buy your retirement RV. You will recover a portion of its purchase price when you buy the next rig, so look at the difference as an investment in your RV education.

Joe: Buy about a 24 to 26-foot trailer or a 28 to 30-foot motorhome. This is a versatile size. It will fit into most government campgrounds yet is large enough to provide the creature comforts you will want for extended periods of time.

Chances are you'll decide on a larger size vehicle for your retirement rig, but you might also discover that this is more than enough RV for your needs. Either way, you'll learn how to make the most out of the space you have.

You'll want the usual electric (30 amp), water and sewer hookup capabilities. If the RV you buy is prewired for cable TV and telephone hookups, all the better.

Some RVers camp self contained most of the time. Others prefer RV parks with full hookups. Most fall somewhere in between. Get an RV with large self-containment capabilities for your learning experience.

There's no such thing as an RV with enough storage space, especially for extended travelers and fulltime RVers.

Be sure you have adequate closet space, cupboards and drawers.

Outside storage bays should be large enough for tools, folding chairs, a grill and other items you don't want to store inside. A rooftop storage pod can be added to carry lightweight items that you will only use occasionally.

Pay close attention to the weight carrying and towing capacities of your training RV. You want as much net cargo-carrying capacity as possible and you don't want to overload your tow vehicle.

If you decide to get a trailer, be sure you have a properly equipped tow vehicle. This could be your present truck or you can buy a decent used one.

If you choose a motorhome, plan on towing a small, lightweight car. A small used car with manual transmission might be the least expensive route to go.

Remember, the plan is to eventually trade in these vehicles and buy the one(s) that will best satisfy your interests and needs.

Shopping for, purchasing, equipping and operating your training RV will give you experience. Experience is the best teacher. It gives the test first and the lesson afterwards.

Vicki: Once you have your RV ready to go, go! Start with a shakedown trip to a nearby RV park or campground with full hookups. Spend one full day and night camping self contained and another day and night with full hookups. Try out all the features of your rig. The objective is to discover any problems and then get them corrected before you take any serious trips.

Most people who are close to retirement age are usually in a position to take an occasional three or four days off and three or four week vacations. Take advantage of these days to spend as much time as possible traveling and camping in your RV.

Go to a new and different campground each trip. Get comfortable with the idea of going into and setting up camp in unfamiliar locations. That's what you will be doing as an RV traveler.

Explore a variety of RV parks and campgrounds. Enjoy the RV resorts. Visit the destination RV parks and campgrounds. Stay overnight in enroute parks. Get familiar with the nationwide chain of KOA campgrounds. Camp in national, state, county and city park campgrounds. Spend an occasional night dry camped in the driveways of out-of-town friends and relatives.

Experiment with long travel days and short travel days. Travel early in the day and get off the road before 3:30 in the afternoon. Travel at night. Experiment. You may be surprised at what you discover.

Pursue your interests and hobbies while on the road. Go fishing. Explore ghost towns. Play golf. Visit flea markets. Follow the races. Visit old friends. Make new ones.

After you and your RV have a little experience, begin taking journeys of two to four months duration. Learn what is involved with actually living on the road.

Use these trips to learn about your RV and RVing. You'll also learn about your personal RVing interests, needs and budget.

Joe: Meanwhile, simplify your everyday life. Start with your home. Who will look after it while you are gone for long periods of time? Who will retrieve and forward your mail? Who can act on your behalf while you are absent? With any luck it will be the same person.

Simplify your yard maintenance. Install sprinklers. Hire a gardener. Replace hard to care for plants with easy care ones.

Simplify your banking and bill paying arrangements. How will you accomplish these chores while you are away from home?

Develop a system of communicating with friends and family while you are on the road. Most extended RV travelers have a telephone calling card for use at pay phones, a telephone answering machine at home for taking messages and a cellular phone in their RV for emergencies. Ask the campgrounds you visit what facilities they have available for e-mail.

These preparations will make the transition to RV retirement a lot easier.

Research. Join RV clubs, attend RV shows, explore RV dealerships, subscribe to RV magazines, read RV books, attend RV seminars, visit with fellow RVers, surf the internet. Learn all you can about the various RVs, RV lifestyles, RV parks, campgrounds, travel destinations and activities.

Vicki: Start now. Become an experienced and knowledgeable RVer. Learn just what your personal interests and needs are.

When retirement time gets closer you'll be able to decide whether you want to be a full-time RVer, an extended traveler, a snowbird, an occasional RV user or a confirmed couch potato.

You'll be in a position to choose the RV that will satisfy your interests and needs. You'll be making an informed decision. Best of all, you'll be taking action to make your dream come true!

Home Security and Maintenance

"You've mentioned that you are on the road for three to four months at a time. What do you do about the security and maintenance of your home while you are gone?"

Joe: It took a while to achieve but our house is as low maintenance as it can get. The yard is landscaped with plants, bushes and trees that require very little care. Weeding and trimming are only necessary about twice a year.

Everything is watered by a sprinkler system on an automatic timer. The sprinklers are timed to come on at about four o'clock in the morning. That way, if the sprinklers come on while it is raining, no one will notice. The sprinklers remain on timers year round and are adjusted according to the needs of the season.

The lawn is mowed weekly by a professional lawn mowing crew. We intentionally scheduled the lawn mowing to occur the day before trash pickup. The mowing crew places the bagged trimmings at the curb for the trash truck and the next day the trimmings are hauled away. The mowing crew comes every week; even when we are at home.

Selected interior and exterior lights are on timers. They go on and off as if we were there. In fact, they remain on timers 365 days of the year. The timers are adjusted periodically to coincide with normal daylight hours.

Mail is collected daily from our curbside mailbox and delivered to our daughter-in-law who then forwards it to us.

The mail collector also picks up throw-away ads, door hangers and any windblown trash whose presence would reveal our absence.

We discontinue and restart newspaper delivery so often we have the phone number on speed dial. By the way, we stop the newspaper at least two days before we leave. Just to make sure it really does stop.

A neighbor parks his car in our driveway.

With the exception of people coming and going, our house maintains the same outward appearance whether we are at home or on the road. We frequently have neighbors who are surprised when they find out we were not at home for the past few months.

Vicki: I used to have a lot of inside house plants. As much as I enjoyed them, they were a bother when we went on the road. At first, we had a relative come inside the house and water them once a week. Then we farmed them out to friends and relatives who were willing to plant sit. But, considering the frequency and the length of time we were gone, both those solutions seemed a real imposition. So I gradually replaced the live plants with silk plants. I did keep a couple of favorites and fortunately our next-door neighbor enjoys plant sitting with them. In fact, they always come back looking healthier than when they left.

I am not going to reveal the specifics of the physical security of our home. Suffice it to say that Joe's law enforcement experience and security management background has a profound influence on the way our house is secured.

It would be difficult to break into our house and almost impossible to break in undetected. Once inside, a burglar's priorities would quickly change from thievery to escape. I suspect my husband has a bit of a mean streak in him.

Joe: Only you can determine the type and extent of security your home should have. There are a few common sense precautions that anyone can implement.

Make your house look occupied so as not to invite burglars. This can be as easy as installing a few inexpensive light timers and arranging for a reliable person to maintain the yard.

Install good locks on your gates, doors and windows. Make it easier to break into your neighbor's house than yours.

Leave a radio on just loud enough to be heard if you listen closely from outside a door or window. You'd be amazed at what a good deterrent this can be.

Put in an alarm system. Its a good idea to discuss this with your local police department first. Ask them what type of system would work best for your circumstances and their response policies. Then have the alarm system installed by a professional alarm company.

It is not enough to just have an alarm go off. What happens then? Will someone respond? Who? How long will it take for them to get to your home? Will they have your permission and the ability to enter the house? Who should they notify if there is a problem? Chances are you won't be able to get home for a couple of days. Who will be responsible for securing your home until you return?

Test and adjust your alarm system to be sure it only activates when it should. False alarms can result in police department fines, discontinued response and your neighbors hoping that you really do get robbed.

Minimize the losses that can occur if someone does burglarize your home. Put your cash and jewelry in a safe deposit box. Hide or secure guns and other easily pawned objects. Make it time consuming and difficult for an intruder to locate and remove your valuables.

Vicki: Our sons and daughters-in-law live nearby. They check our house periodically. A quick walk through reveals anything unusual. One of our sons also checks to make sure the alarm system, lights, sprinklers and timers are all working properly.

The neighbors know both our sons and their wives. They have their phone numbers. The neighbors have been asked to call our sons if they see anything unusual around our house.

Both of our sons are authorized to write checks on one of our checking accounts. This gives them the ability to pay for any emergency repairs that may be necessary.

As you can see, most of our home security and maintenance arrangements remain the same whether we are at home or on the road. When it's time to leave, we notify our sons, mail collector, newspaper and immediate neighbors. A few additional security precautions are put in place and off we go.

Now, if you live in a secured condominium complex, you might have very different considerations; like, how do you keep the pipes from freezing or ...

Banking and Bill Paying

"We're planning to take a series of three and four month trips beginning next summer. What preparations would you suggest we make for banking and paying our bills while we are away from home?"

Vicki: Start now, it takes time to identify the things you need to change and it takes time to implement those changes.

RVers who plan to spend more than a few weeks on the road usually have to find a way to deal with their banking and bill-paying responsibilities while they are away from home.

One method is to estimate and prepay the bills that will come due while you are absent. But, that can take cash out of interest earning accounts sooner than necessary.

Another approach is to have all your statements and bills forwarded to you by mail, then pay them as you do at home. But, chances are you will not receive your forwarded mail until at least a week after it has been delivered to your home. That means income will be deposited later than necessary and some bills could get paid late.

An easier alternative is to develop a simplified banking and bill paying system that will take care of your financial obligations not only while you are at home, but while you are on the road as well.

Ideally, such a system will minimize your need to go to the bank, minimize the amount of cash you need to carry, minimize the number of checks you have to write, and minimize the number of statements and bills you receive in the mail

You can begin to simplify your banking needs by consolidating as many of your financial affairs as possible at one financial institution. This will reduce the number of statements you receive in the mail.

Check out the services offered by banks, savings and loans, credit unions and even the brokerage houses. You probably won't need a personal relationship with your banker, so choose a financial institution that offers:

Interest-earning checking account. Many financial institutions offer a free checking account when a minimum amount of money is maintained in either the checking account or some type of savings account. The alternative seems to be a checking account that charges you a fee for the privilege of the bank using your money.

Overdraft protection. This allows you to write a check for more money (within limits) than you have in your checking account. The financial institution automatically advances or loans you the amount necessary to cover the difference. Overdraft protection provides a temporary fix in case a bookkeeping error results in you writing a check that exceeds your balance. It can also be the source of an emergency loan.

ATM card. Get an ATM card that is associated with a large network such as Cirrus, Plus or Star. An ATM card allows you to get cash just about everywhere you travel. No need to carry large amounts of cash on your person or in your RV. And, you will not have any need for traveler's checks either.

Visa or MasterCard. These credit cards are universally accepted by just about every type of merchant. Having one (or both) of these cards allows you to eliminate all those individual merchant credit cards that clutter up your wallet and fill your mailbox with monthly statements.

Debit card. A debit card is utilized just like a credit card except that the amount of the transaction is immediately deducted from your checking (or savings) account.

Electronic deposit of income. You can arrange to have most regular sources of income such as pay checks, retirement checks or social security checks, electronically deposited to your checking or savings account.

If, for example, a check is due on the first of the month, it is electronically deposited to your account on the first of the month. No waiting for the checks to arrive, no filling out deposit slips, no going to the bank.

Electronic payment of bills. You can also arrange to have your regular monthly bills, such as mortgage payments, car payments and utility bills automatically and electronically paid each month. The money is withdrawn from your checking or savings account. When the statement arrives in the mail it will say something like "Statement Only, Do Not Pay." No waiting for the bill to arrive, no writing and mailing checks, no late charges.

Telephone banking services. By dialing an 800 number from anywhere in the country you can determine the latest deposits, withdrawals and balances of your various accounts. You can move money from one account to the other. Funds can be kept in interest bearing accounts until they are needed in your checking account.

Internet banking services. Go on the internet, bring up your financial institution's web site, enter your access code and you can see (and print out) the history and status of your accounts. No need to wait for your monthly statement to get forwarded to you in the mail. You can also instruct the financial institution's computer to move money from one account to another. You will find that internet access is available in most of today's RV parks and campgrounds.

Bank by mail Most financial institutions will provide you with deposit slips and envelopes so you can deposit checks by mail.

Safe-deposit box Get a large enough safe-deposit box so you can safely store any small valuables you do not want to leave at home when you travel.

Joe: Here is a suggestion of how you can use these services to develop a simple, yet consistent, banking and bill paying system:

Minimize your need to go to the bank by: banking by telephone; banking by internet; and banking by mail. Arrange to have your income electronically deposited. Electronic deposit eliminates the concern about checks lost in the mail, checks being forwarded in the mail and deposits not getting to the bank on time.

Minimize the number and expense of writing and mailing checks by automatically and electronically paying as many bills as possible (loans, utilities, etc.). Electronic payment assures you that, whether you are at home or on the road, your bills will be paid on time.

Minimize the amount of cash you need to carry by: writing checks; using your credit card; or using your debit card instead of paying cash.

When you are traveling, use your debit or credit card for as many financial transactions as possible. Purchase fuel, pay for campgrounds and buy groceries using your credit card. By the way, when you pay for groceries with a debit card, most stores will allow you to obtain cash as well. This can eliminate visits to ATMs and paying ATM fees.

Instead of waiting for your credit-card statement to be forwarded while you are on the road, go on line with your credit card company or call the Customer Service 800 number on the back of your credit card. Find out your balance or minimum payment and send them a check. If the credit card is with your financial institution, you can make payment by using the 800 number or online banking system.

Another option to waiting for your monthly credit card statement to be forwarded, is to add up the credit card receipts you have generated and write a check for the amount due.

You can also arrange to have your credit card payment automatically and electronically deducted from your bank account.

Minimize your ATM visits (and fees) by obtaining at least a week's worth of cash whenever you make an ATM withdrawal.

Minimize the number of statements and bills you receive in the mail and the number of checks you have to write by using only one financial institution and one credit card. Pay the credit card balance before interest charges are levied.

It may take a little thought and planning, but you should be able to develop a simplified, yet consistent banking and bill paying system that will take care of your financial obligations not only while you are at home, but while you are on the road as well.

Receiving Mail

"How do I arrange to have mail forwarded to me when I am on the road?"

Joe: The biggest challenge you have is to find a reliable person who is willing to retrieve your mail from your home mail box and forward it to you while you are on the road. Perhaps the person who is looking after your house will also be willing to forward your mail. Tell them you will call periodically to let them know where it should be sent.

When you are ready to receive mail, look at a map and locate a small town that you will be traveling through in about five days. Ask your mail forwarder to put all your mail into a single envelope and to address it as follows:

> Your Name
> c/o General Delivery
> City or Town, State, Zip Code

The receiving post office will hold your mail for ten days before returning it to the sender. All you have to do to retrieve your mail is show the postal clerk your personal identification.

Here are a few tips to make things work smoothly. Select a small town to receive your mail. You, the tourist, will have an easier time locating the post office. You will also find it easier to locate a parking place for your RV in a small town. Our experience is that small town post offices seem to keep better track of general delivery mail.

Get a *Zip Code Directory* from the post office or a book store. Not only will it provide you with each town's zip code, you will be able to tell how small a town it is. The fewer zip codes in town, the fewer post office branches.

Not all post office banches will receive and hold general delivery mail. Once you have decided where you would like to receive your mail, call the post office at 1-800-ASK-USPS (1-800-275-8777). They will tell you which post office branch in that town can receive general delivery mail. They will also tell you that post office's zip code, their street address and, in some cases, give you directions on how to get there.

Vicki: Ask your mail forwarder to send your mail via the US Post Office's Priority Mail. It will usually arrive in two to three days. We have waited as long as five days on a couple of occasions, however.

Be specific as to what mail you want forwarded to you, what you want saved for your return and what can be thrown away.

Make life easy for your mail forwarding friend by providing a postal scale, a supply of (Priority Mail) envelopes and sufficient stamps or postage money.

Your mail forwarder can stuff the Priority Mail flat rate envelope with as much mail as it will hold and send it to any town in the United States. Remind your mail forwarder, however, that any envelope weighing more than one pound must be personally handed to a postal employee.

You might be able to receive your mail at a campground or RV park where you are staying. Ask the owner or manager if they will let you do this, some campgrounds do not want the responsibility of handling your mail. It is a good idea to have your mail forwarder note your arrival date on the lower left corner of the envelope, just in case the envelope arrives before you do.

Medical Care And Prescriptions

"What if I need medical attention while traveling? What do I do about getting my prescriptions filled?"

Joe: RV travelers should be happy to learn that good medical care and prescription refills are available just about everywhere they go. A little planning and research makes them easy to obtain.

Start out by anticipating and preparing for any potential medical problems that may be encountered during your trip.

Talk to your health insurer or HMO. Find out what procedures you should follow to obtain emergency and routine medical care while you are away from home. In most cases, you will be covered if you follow their guidelines.

If you wear prescription glasses, take a spare pair with you. And, it doesn't hurt to take a copy of the prescription, just in case. That way, if you need to get another pair along the way, you can take your existing prescription into one of the quick eyeglass centers to get new glasses instead of having to make an appointment with an optometrist for an eye examination.

If you are under the regular care of a physician, before leaving on an extended trip, make an appointment with your doctor. Tell him about the trip you'll be taking. Make sure there is no medical reason to postpone it. If your doctor feels that you should visit another doctor along the way, ask for a referral.

Ask your doctor whether or not your medical condition would make it advisable to take a copy of your medical records with you. If so, allow plenty of time for the copying to be done. Keep in mind that, although it is possible to fax your medical records across the country, you may find yourself in a situation where you need a copy of your records on Friday night and your doctor's office doesn't open until the following Monday morning.

If necessary, ask the doctor to prescribe a sufficient quantity of medication to last the duration of your trip. It may be possible for the doctor to prescribe a one-to-three month supply of medicine and authorize two or three refills on that same prescription.

The most important thing to be aware of when you have prescriptions to fill is that, in most cases, a prescription is good only in the state in which it is written. Do not count on being able to take a prescription written by a doctor in your home state into a pharmacy in another state to have it filled.

If you are taking a non-narcotic medication, ask your hometown pharmacist to give you your prescription and one or two of the authorized refills in a sufficient quantity to last your entire trip. Store the medicine in a cool, dark place in your RV and it should travel with no problem.

If your pharmacy or insurance company does not allow a several-month quantity to be filled at one time, or if you are taking a narcotic medication that, by law, cannot be dispensed in large quantities, you'll need to explore some other options.

Perhaps you can get your original prescription filled at your hometown pharmacy. Then, when you are ready for a refill, you could ask a relative, friend or neighbor to get the prescription refilled for you. Maybe the person who is forwarding your mail can enclose your refill in your next envelope of mail.

Check into the mail order pharmacies. You will find them advertised on the internet and in travel and RV magazines. You send a completed form along with your prescription and payment to the mail order pharmacy; they then mail the medication to you. When you are comparing mail order companies, ask for a list of the states they can and cannot mail prescriptions to. They may not be able to mail to every state.

Many extended RV travelers use nation-wide, chain pharmacies such as those at Wal-Mart and K-Mart. They get their original prescription filled at their hometown Wal-Mart. When it's time for a refill, they go into another Wal-Mart with the number on their prescription bottle. The pharmacist feeds the number into the computer and the refill order is processed.

Before relying on a chain pharmacy to get medication while on the road, it is always a good idea to check with the one in your hometown. There may be laws affecting their ability to transfer prescriptions from one store or state to another.

There are times when you may require medical treatment while traveling. If you have a medical emergency, don't hesitate. Go to an emergency hospital. Look for a big blue sign with a white "H". You'll see them along the interstates, highways and even in downtown areas. When you see that sign, you'll know that an emergency medical facility is at the next off ramp or right down the road. If you don't see a hospital nearby, ask a policeman, fireman or anyone else in the area where the nearest emergency medical facility is located. Rather than just giving you directions, they may lead you there.

If your medical problem is not a real emergency, do not go to an emergency hospital. You'll have to wait while they take care of the genuine emergencies, and they will probably charge you more than a doctor's office would for the same treatment.

If you need the services of a doctor or a dentist and it's not an emergency, ask someone who works or lives in the area for a recommendation. If you are staying in a campground, don't overlook the obvious--ask someone at the campground office. They will very likely give you the name and phone number of their own doctor. You will be getting a first-hand recommendation.

You could also drive around the area surrounding a hospital. You'll usually find medical offices located in the neighborhood. If the doctor's receptionist tells you the doctor is not taking any new patients, tell her you are a traveler and do not want to become a regular patient. It might also help if you offer to pay by cash or credit card rather than through your medical insurance company.

Many RV travelers report having excellent results with the emergency, walk-in medical clinics. These clinics are located in even the smallest towns and are usually easy to find. Some of them advertise on the campground maps that you are given when you register. And, of course, you will find them in the telephone book "Yellow Pages" listed under "Medical". Many of these relatively small clinics are surprisingly well equipped and amazingly efficient. They usually have their own x-ray facilities and labs and are staffed with conscientious doctors, nurses and clerical personnel.

If one of your traveling party is ever hospitalized, ask the hospital if you can park your RV in the hospital parking lot. A number of RVers report that not only were they allowed to stay in their RVs in the parking lot, but in many cases they were even directed to a secure site where they could hook up to electricity.

Medical care and medicine are available just about everywhere you go. A little planning and preparation on your part will just make them easier to obtain.

Telephone Communications

"How do RVers keep in touch with their families while they are traveling? Should we carry a cellular telephone?"

Joe: Telephone communication while traveling is easily accomplished thanks to a variety of modern-day services and equipment.

Telephone hookups are available at some RV parks. Typically, the local telephone company activates the connection and assigns you a telephone number. This service, obviously, is designed for those who intend to remain at the RV park for a period of time.

A growing number of RV parks, however, (especially the newer ones) are beginning to offer telephone hookups at their sites on a daily basis. A telephone hookup means you can place and receive calls and use your computer to go on line. You simply request and pay for the telephone hookup just as you would an electric, water or cable connection.

Pay phones can be found everywhere you go. Chances are, most of your on-the-road telephone calls will be made from pay phones.

Always make sure you access your own long-distance carrier before placing a telephone call. This way you'll avoid the outrageous fees some telephone companies charge unsuspecting customers.

Telephone calling cards are a convenient way to place long-distance calls. You can get one from the larger RV clubs, your local telephone service provider or from a long-distance carrier such as AT&T, MCI or Sprint. While there won't be a monthly service fee, some telephone calling cards add a surcharge for each call you place. Shop around.

By the way, don't let anyone see or hear you using your calling card number. If they are able to copy it, they can place calls that will show up on your telephone bill.

Prepaid phone cards are another way to save money on long-distance calls. You'll find them for sale in department stores, supermarkets and drug stores.

When you purchase a prepaid phone card, you buy a given amount of telephone calling time, usually expressed in minutes.

You can make your calls any time, any day and to any place in the continental United States with a prepaid phone card and the cost per minute is the same. This can be an economical advantage if you want to place long-distance calls during the daytime hours.

Do some comparison shopping. We've seen the cost vary from a high of forty cents per minute on one company's card to a low of six cents per minute on another company's card. Obviously, you want the card with the lowest cost per minute.

Be sure you buy from a reputable source and check to see if the card has an expiration date. You don't want to buy a card you can't use.

Vicki: Telephone answering machines allow people to leave messages for you when they call your home telephone. You can retrieve and respond to those messages while you are on the road.

Invest in a quality telephone answering machine. Get one with a "remote retrieval" feature. This will allow you to call home while you are on the road and instruct your answering machine to relay your messages to you.

Another answering machine feature, one that will save you money, is called "tollsaver." By flicking a switch on the answering machine you instruct it to answer your phone on the first ring if anyone has left a message for you but to wait until the fourth ring if there are not any messages.

When you call home and your phone rings more than two times, you can assume there are no messages on the answering machine. You can save the cost of a toll call by hanging up before the answering machine answers the phone on the fourth ring.

When you return home, a flick of a switch instructs your machine to return to its normal answering mode.

By the way, don't invite any burglars by announcing on your answering machine that you are away from home.

Voice mail service may be offered by your local telephone company. This service is similar to an answering machine except the equipment is owned and operated by the telephone company. The phone company doesn't offer any kind of "toll saver" feature in conjunction with its voice-mail service

Commercial voice mail services advertise in RV magazines. RV clubs that offer mail forwarding usually offer some form of message service for a moderate fee.

Emergency telephone message service is offered to the members of some RV and automobile travel clubs as a benefit of membership. Typically, the caller dials an 800 number to leave an emergency message and the member dials an 800 number to retrieve the message. A service like this can be worth the price of a club's annual membership.

Joe: **Cellular telephones** allow you to place or receive telephone calls in nearly all populated areas and along most major highways throughout the USA and Canada.

RV travelers with cellular phones feel secure knowing they can call for help in an emergency. They also have peace of mind knowing their families can reach them if there is an emergency at home.

Cellular service charges, however, can mount up quickly. In addition to a monthly service fee, be prepared to pay for each minute of phone usage (airtime) for both incoming and outgoing calls.

When you leave your "home" cellular company's area and travel into the geographical area of another cellular company, you become a "roamer". Generally, a "roamer's" fee is charged once on any day a cellular call is placed or received.

Additionally, a "roamer" might be charged for airtime.

"Roamers" can also expect to pay long-distance charges whenever they place or receive a long-distance call. When callers dial your cellular phone number they are charged only for the standard telephone call to your "home" cellular area. You are charged for the long-distance call from your "home" cellular area to your present location.

You can control your cellular costs by limiting the number of cellular calls (both incoming and outgoing) and the amount of time spent on the cellular phone. One way to do this is to minimize the number of people who know your cellular phone number

Consider starting out with the cellular company's economy plan and with only one or two close family members knowing your cellular phone number. Later, if you want a more expensive plan, the cellular company should be happy to oblige you, and you can always add to the list of those who have your cellular phone number.

Investigate the "One-Rate" plans offered by many cellular services. You pay a monthly fee for a given number of airtime minutes but there might not be any roaming or long-distance charges.

Vicki: Pagers can reach you anywhere, anytime. The caller dials your pager number, waits for a tone, then enters the number they want you to call. Your pager beeps and displays your caller's number. Some paging systems can relay entire messages and even e-mail.

Visit a telecommunication store for more details. Be sure they understand you will be traveling out of your local area. It makes a difference in the type and cost of service.

Keep in mind that while the pager can reach you, you still have to locate a telephone in order to reply.

Some RV travelers have their callers reach them by pager. They can then decide whether to reply by using their cellular phone or the next convenient pay phone. This method allows RV travelers to control their cellular phone costs. It also helps guard against having their cellular phone cloned (by turning the cellular phone off between calls).

Most RV travelers have found that the calling card, answering machine, and a cellular phone (economy plan and used only for emergencies) are more than adequate for their telephone needs.

Computers and RVs

"Can I take my computer in my RV? Do I need to be aware of anything special? Does anyone make computer furniture for RVs? Will I be able to go on line?"

Joe: Yes, you can take your computer in your RV. Yes, computer desks are available for RVs. Yes, you can go online. And yes, there are a few simple considerations.

The first thing to consider is where you are going to put the computer and all its peripheral equipment. Chances are you'll also be lugging along a printer, connecting cables, modem, disks and manuals.

A built-in computer desk seems to make sense. That way you have a place for everything and everything can stay in its place.

A number of RV manufacturers offer built-in computer desks as an option in some of their models. If you are shopping for a new rig, ask the dealer if one is available for the RV you are considering.

Most of the RV computer desks we have seen were created by the RV owner. All of these custom desks involved removing or altering some of the RV's original furnishings.

Some simply amounted to the installation of a small desk purchased at a furniture store. Others were constructed by bridging a couple of two-drawer file cabinets with some kind of a writing surface. The clever ones were those that served more than one purpose.

In most cases, a bungee cord or adjustable strap secured the computer and printer to the desk top during travel. A thick felt pad or piece of foam under the equipment dampened road vibration.

Most computer-toting RVers set up their monitors, computers and printers on an existing flat surface such as the dashboard, second table or even the kitchen table. Obviously, a place has to be found to secure these items when they are not being used, especially while traveling.

A popular solution for those who are unable or unwilling to make room inside their closets or cupboards is to seatbelt their computer equipment onto couches and chairs while traveling.

Vicki: You didn't say whether your computer is a desktop model or laptop. Both seem to do well in RVs. If you are contemplating the purchase of a computer for use in an RV, we would suggest you seriously consider the advantages of a laptop.

A laptop computer is designed to withstand some of the jolts and bumps of being carried and moved from place to place. It takes up considerably less room than a desktop and, as its name implies, it doesn't require a dedicated workspace.

We gave a lot of thought to working on the road when we purchased our most recent computer. We wanted something that would travel well, take up a minimum of space and could be easily carried between our house and the RV. While the idea of a computer desk appealed to us, we were reluctant to sacrifice the furniture and space it would take.

We purchased a laptop computer and a notebook size printer. Computer, printer, cords and cables all fit into a briefcase. A versatile folding table, 16 inches by 32 inches, provides additional desktop area when needed. The table stores flush against the end wall inside our wardrobe closet when not in use.

We especially appreciate the portability of the laptop. It has the ability to operate on a variety of power sources; regular electricity, plugged into a cigar lighter or using its own built-in battery. That means we can use it at the kitchen table, in the passenger seat or while sitting in a lawn chair.

I frequently work with our laptop sitting in my lap as we drive on interstates (and you know how smooth they are). I haven't experienced any problems.

During a trip to Alaska, one of our caravan members, a writer, worked on her desktop computer while her husband drove. To my knowledge, they never encountered any computer problems either.

Be careful, though, if you plan to use your computer while traveling. As I understand it, the hard-drive's read/write head rides on a cushion of air while operating. We have been told that a good jolt could bring the head into contact with the hard-drive and cause it to crash. This is one more reason to back up your computer's hard drive.

By the way, generator and campground power is subject to surges, spikes and other aggravations. Be sure to use a surge protector when operating your computer and printer.

Joe: Going online while traveling is still an adventure for RVers. The simplest way is to stay at one of the rare campgrounds that offers telephone hookups at each site.

Another option is to ask the campground operator if there is a telephone jack in the office that you can use to retrieve your e-mail. Expect a mixed bag of responses to that request.

Do ask about the availability of telephone jacks and hookups. More and more campground owners are installing the appropriate facilities as they become aware of the needs of today's computer-oriented RVers.

Vicki: Computers are very much a part of today's RVing experience. Internet sites provide information about choosing, using and maintaining your rig. Programs are available to help map your trip, locate fuel stops and select campgrounds. And computer games can occupy a bored child on a rainy day. But please, don't let the computer become a substitute for the family sitting around a campfire, cooking marshmallows, telling tales and singing songs.

E-Mail On The Road

"Will I be able to connect to the internet and receive e-mail while I am traveling in my RV?"

Joe: Connecting to the internet while traveling in an RV is a bit of a challenge. Telephone connections are just not available in every campground.

But... computers, the internet and e-mail are here to stay. They have become as important to our everyday lives as televisions and telephones. RVers are telling campground owners that accessing their e-mail is important and, to their credit, the campground owners are responding.

Many new RV parks and resorts are including telephone hookups at each campsite in their construction plans. An increasing number of established campgrounds, while unable to justify the expense of retrofitting all their sites with telephone hookups, are installing telephone jacks in their offices, lounges or laundry rooms for the use of their guests.

Understanding (and business savvy) campground operators are generously disconnecting their fax machines long enough for campers to plug in and download their e-mail.

Still, access to e-mail at campgrounds remains sketchy. So, if it is important to you, before you register, ask if the campground has facilities for you to get your e-mail.

Vicki: There are other ways to do your e-mail on the road. A number of RVers use an acoustic coupler to connect their laptops to payphones so they can do their e-mailing. Some folks think they are just great, others tell us that trying to juggle a laptop, telephone instrument and acoustic coupler while swatting at mosquitoes in a cramped phone booth is just too much trouble.

RVers have discovered that the restaurants in many of the large travel plazas (formally known as truck stops) have telephone jacks at the perimeter tables. Some, like the Flying J Travel Plazas, have sit-down booths with a telephone jack for laptop users. Ask the restaurant's cashier or the person at the fuel desk if they have facilities for you to plug in your laptop.

Hotel and motel lobbies frequently have telephone jacks available. They are usually located among the payphones.

The telephone jacks located in campground offices, hotel lobbies and on the tables of travel plazas are intended for brief usage only. The idea is to go on line, send your prepared e-mail, download your incoming e-mail and get off the line. These connections are not intended for the folks who want to surf the net, go into chat rooms or research their family's genealogy.

Joe: If you need to spend more time on line here are a few suggestions.

The campground telephone jacks are usually not busy before 4:00 pm and after 10:00 pm. You may be able to spend some time on line during the non-busy hours without inconveniencing other campers.

Many public libraries have computers available for the public to access the internet, usually at no charge. You may have to reserve a block of time at some of the busier libraries, though.

Kinkos fast-print shops are nationwide and open 24-hours a day, seven days a week.. They advertise PC and Mac rental stations. For a nominal fee you can send and receive e-mail. For an hourly rate you can access the internet.

If you want to access the internet from your RV, you'll have to stay in RV parks that offer telephone hookups at their campsites. Unfortunately, only a small percentage of RV parks offer telephone hookups and many of those are restricted to long-term guests. Those RV parks that do have telephone hookups at individual campsites are rarely what you would refer to as budget campgrounds. Their rates typically reflect the type of facilities they offer.

The *Trailer Life RV Park and Campground Directory* tells you which RV parks and campgrounds are modem friendly. The campground listings indicate whether the telephone hookups are located at individual campsites or a telephone jack in the office. You can also go to the TL directory website (www.tldirectory.com) and, by typing in the name of a city or town and specifying "modem friendly," locate those campgrounds where you will be able to access the internet.

By the way, the TL Directory website also provides you with a link to those RV parks and campgrounds that have websites.

Vicki: We suggest you sign up with an internet service provider (ISP) that provides local telephone access numbers in cities and towns around the country. Ideally, your ISP will also have an 800 number to use when a local number is not available.

There are other, more expensive options. It is possible to go on line using cellular or satellite telephones. We've tried them. They work, but they are pricey.

Accessing e-mail and connecting to the internet is just another RV travel adventure. Go for it!

Choosing An RV For Extended Travel

"We want to spend several months each year traveling around the country. What's the best RV for us?"

Joe: Lately, we are hearing that question at almost every RV seminar we present. It would appear that more and more folks are becoming extended RV travelers like us.

Typical extended RV travelers go out in their RV for six to twelve weeks at a time. They may take two or three trips and accumulate 10,000 or more miles a year.

While, essentially, they are on vacation, extended travelers live in their RVs just like fulltimers do. Since they encounter all kinds of weather conditions, their RV wardrobe will range from summer shorts to down jackets and raincoats. It will also include grubbies, casual wear and semi-dressy outfits (with shoes to match).

Extended RV travelers occasionally like to prepare regular home-cooked meals like spaghetti with meat sauce or roast beef and mashed potatoes. They spend more evenings inside their RVs watching television, reading or working on their computer than they do sitting outside next to a campfire.

Extended RV travelers may ask their rigs to climb the Rocky Mountains, cross the southwestern deserts and follow the Alaska Highway. They encounter temperatures from freezing to 120 degrees. Self-containment features are frequently every bit as important as the convenience of hookups.

The ideal rig for an extended RV traveler combines a perfect blend of easy mobility, copious cargo capacity and comfortable living accommodations.

Vicki: The question of whether to get a motorhome or trailer comes first. This is a personal choice with a lot of considerations. Either will do the job.

When we were weekending and vacationing, we had small travel trailers and then a Class C motorhome. They were space efficient, would go anywhere and their price tags were proportionate to the amount of time we spent using them.

If we were to become fulltimers we would give serious consideration to a large conventional or fifth-wheel trailer.

But, as extended RV travelers, we chose a Class A motorhome because it is easy to drive, back and level. That's important when manuevering in and out of RV parks is almost a daily occurrence.

Class A motorhomes offer comfortable, spacious interiors. Their large outside storage bays are capable of carrying everything we need.

The size of an extended RV traveler's rig is a compromise between interior living comfort and the ability of the RV to fit into the places you want to go. Let's face it, a 40-foot motorhome is more comfortable to live in than a van conversion; the van, however, can go anywhere while the 40- foot motorhome has limitations.

Our personal travels take us to national parks, RV resorts and a variety of commercial and government campgrounds. We have also spent a fair amount of time camped in friends' driveways and the parking lots of RV shows. As a result, we have come to the conclusion that a motorhome between 32 and 36 feet is about the right compromise for our extended RV travel needs.

Joe: Gasoline or diesel? We have driven both gasoline and diesel powered motorhomes across the country. On each of those occasions we were towing a compact car with all four wheels on the ground. This may come as a surprise to many, but we found the performance and capabilities of both the big block V-8 and the 5.9 turbo-charged diesel to be pretty much the same.

The diesel pusher chassis had a significantly higher cargo carrying capacity. It was smoother, quieter, and got better mileage. But the gasoline rig did the job very nicely and the price tag was significantly lower.

The diesel chassis definitely has the advantage when it comes to durability and longevity. If you know you will be extended RV travelers for some time to come. If you think you will put 10,000 miles or more per year on your RV. If your budget can handle the price tag. It makes sense to go with the diesel.

You'll want to tow a small transportation car or truck. Be sure the motorhome is capable of handling the weight.

Extended RV travelers carry lots of stuff. An RV with 3,000 pounds or more of cargo carrying capacity is ideal. Not every RV has this kind of cargo carrying capacity, but they're out there.

One manufacturer, for example, recently introduced an entry level, diesel motorhome with a net carrying capacity of slightly over 5,000 pounds and the capability of towing an additional 5,000 pounds. They also did a dynamite job of weight distribution. Side to side weight variance is less than 250 pounds.

Self-containment capacities are important to extended RV travelers. An 80 to 100-gallon fresh-water tank will provide up to a week's worth of water for two people. An equal size gray-water holding tank is desirable but may not be easy to find.

You'll find that 35 to 40 gallons of black-water holding tank capacity is sufficient for a week of self-contained camping.

We have determined that twin 6-volt batteries, a 2,000 watt inverter and a 6,500 watt generator meet all of our electrical needs while camping self-contained.

A 20 to 25-gallon propane tank will do the job. During really cold weather we have consumed up to a gallon of propane per day, a good deal less during summertime.

A combination gas/electric water heater will save a considerable amount of propane when you have an electric hookup.

Dual pane windows and good insulation will help keep cold weather at bay.

Torque windows in the bedroom will permit cross ventilation when it's raining.

Two roof air-conditioning units, a high-powered roof-vent fan and awnings on all the windows provide relief from the hot sun.

Roof-vent covers make it possible to open the roof vents even though it is raining. We can also drive down the highway with our roof vent open and know the cap won't blow off.

Hydraulic levelers for a motorhome or electric tongue jack for a trailer are real back savers and make leveling and stabilizing an RV faster and easier.

Vicki: RV travelers spend a lot of time inside their rigs. Be sure you get a livable floorplan.

Kitchens located at the front or rear of the rig are usually larger than those located in the center. They also have the advantage of being out of the RV's traffic path.

Many trailer owners have observed that the smoothest riding portion of the trailer is in the front. They prefer to have the kitchen and its breakables located forward of the rear axle.

Rear baths can be large and private but guests sleeping in the front of the RV may disturb the bedroom occupants when they need to use the bathroom.

Split, center baths can also be spacious but may block passage from one end of the RV to the other when they are occupied.

Side-aisle, center baths are accessible from both ends of the RV and don't block traffic, but they frequently are not as spacious as the other plans.

One floorplan offers a compromise by placing the commode and bathroom sink in a small room on one side of the RV and the shower across the hall.

Most RVers appreciate a bedroom that can be closed off from the rest of the RV. It provides privacy for changing clothes and accommodates occupants with different bedtime schedules.

Try the RV on to see if it fits. Sit down in the living area. Would you be comfortable spending an evening in that couch or chair? Are the lights adequate for reading? Where will you place your snack, cold drink and the TV remote control? Is the television easily viewed from every seat?

Convert the couch into a bed. Lie down on both sides. Is it comfortable? A six-foot person would appreciate a bed that is at least 74 inches long. Is the storage area under the couch easily accessible?

A free-standing kitchen table and chairs look homey, are easier to get in and out of and give the RV a spacious appearance. A bench seat dinette, on the other hand, provides underseat storage, the availability of a guest bed and you don't have to secure any chairs before you travel.

How much countertop is available for meal preparation? A side-by-side refrigerator, icemaker and combination microwave/convection oven are all very nice but you need counter space to prepare a meal and stack dirty dishes.

If the kitchen table is located opposite the kitchen counter, it will be convenient for use during meal preparation.

Kitchen sinks should be deep enough to wash your largest pot. The sinks in some RVs take up more counter top area than in others, yet their usable interior dimensions are the same.

Consider how important a propane oven may be to you. A microwave/convection oven can do the same job as a propane oven but may not be operable when you are camping without electric hookups. If the propane oven isn't important, take the large storage space in its place.

Refrigerator interiors generally seem pretty satisfactory. Measure to be sure they will be able to carry one-quart containers of milk, fat jars of pickles and tall bottles of salad dressing. Or plan on transferring these items to smaller containers.

Does the side-by-side refrigerator offer the same (or more) practical carrying capacity as the standard over-and-under refrigerator? Would you rather have the extra freezer capacity of a side-by-side refrigerator or would you prefer the slide-out pantry that may accompany a standard over-and-under refrigerator?

Check the slideout pantry. It may look big but will it accommodate boxes of cold cereal and bags of potato chips or just small sizes of canned goods?

Be sure there is adequate cupboard space for skillets, pans, toaster, coffee pot, crock pot, bowls, dishes and all the other kitchen paraphernalia you'll be taking on the road. Will the height and depth of your cupboards accommodate the size of these items?

Where will the trash container go?

Linoleum or tile on the kitchen floor and under the kitchen table allows easy cleanup.

A queen-size, island bed is easy to get in and out of. If two of you will be sleeping in that bed, both of you should lie down on the bed at the same time. Will you be comfortable on that bed night after night for months at a time?

Measure the RV's mattress and see if form-fitting sheets are available. Not all RV mattresses have the same dimensions as those in your house.

Here are the standard mattress sizes according to a mattress manufacturer:

California King	72" by 84"
Eastern King	76" by 80"
Queen	60" by 80"
Full	53" by 74"
Twin	38" by 74"

There's nothing wrong with a mattress that isn't a standard size, but you do want to make an informed decision.

It doesn't make sense to hang your clothes neatly in a closet only to have the bottom six inches laying rumpled on the closet floor. Compare the interior measurements of the RV's wardrobe closet to the measurement of the garments you expect to hang in that closet.

At home, measure from the top of the clothes rod to the bottom of the longest item of clothing you expect to hang in your RV's closet. Next, measure the shoulder width of the widest clothes you will hang in your RV's closet. Finally, measure from the top of your clothes rod to the bottom of the shirts and slacks you have on hangers.

In the RV, measure the depth of the RV's closet and the distance from the top of the RV's clothes rod to the floor of the closet

Use these measurements to determine if the RV's clothes closets and shirt lockers will accommodate the clothes you wish to take.

You'll be bringing clothes for a variety of temperatures and weather conditions. Be sure there is enough closet, drawer and cupboard space for your clothes.

Most drawer items will fit one way or the other, but some RVs have more drawers with larger dimensions.

Open every drawer. You'd will be surprised at how short some of them can be. Compare the number and size of the drawers in the kitchen, bedroom and bathroom of every prospective rig. We saw one RV that had no drawers for clothes storage. The designer obviously does not wear socks or underwear.

Check out the bathroom. Is the medicine cabinet deep enough and are its shelves high enough to accommodate the items you plan to put in it?

Some folks install a short barrier on each medicine cabinet shelf to prevent the contents from spilling out after a day on the road. Is the medicine cabinet deep enough for you to do the same?

Sit on the commode. Do your knees press up to the wall or bathroom door? Is the toilet paper accessible?

Take your shoes off and step into the shower. Go through the motions of taking a shower and washing your hair. Can you accomplish this without bruising your knuckles on the ceiling or getting wrapped up in the shower curtain?

Be reasonable, most RV showers won't compare to the one you have at home, but do measure and compare the various RV showers available for the type and size rig you are looking at.

Is the bathroom vent located where it can exhaust the steam from the shower?

If the towel holders that come with the RV are insufficient or too small, you can install your own. But where? Measure the available wall or door space.

Be sure there are plenty of conveniently located electrical outlets throughout the RV.

Try everything on for size. Keep in mind that the minor inconveniences you are able to tolerate during a brief vacation can become serious aggravations on a long trip.

The best RV for extended travel, just as for vacationing or fulltiming, is the one that will take you where you want to go and let you do the things you want to do.

Slideout Rooms

"We're writing to you with the hope that some of your readers will assist my wife and I by providing us with information about slideouts in RVs. My wife loves the extra room but I am aware of the weight differences that the slideout adds to the coach.

My biggest concerns center around the possibilities of water, air and exhaust fumes leaking into the coach. Will there be noises and rattles? How about system failures? We are looking forward to the experienced words of wisdom from readers with RV slideouts."

Joe: We published this question and asked our readers to respond. Surprisingly, we did not receive many negative comments about slideouts. Those who wrote were especially enthusiastic about the additional interior space and seemed pleased with the performance of their slideout-equipped trailers and motorhomes. They were also generous with their advice.

As part of our decidedly non-technical research, Vicki and I evaluated a 37-foot, slideout-equipped, gasoline powered motorhome. We traveled and lived in it for two weeks. We also looked closely at a number of trailers and motorhomes with a variety of slideout rooms and mechanisms.

According to those who wrote, the manufacturers have satisfactorily dealt with the problems of dust, fumes and moisture leaking into the coach. Slideout owners emphasized, however, the importance of good seals around the slide opening. Good advice. One RV we looked at had daylight showing between the wall of the extended slide and the floor of the coach.

Look for two sets of seals. One for the extended position and the other for retracted. See if the seals "squeegee" the water from the walls and roof as the room retracts.

Owners also recommended equipping the RV with a "slide topper," an awning that keeps water, dirt and twigs from collecting on the roof of the slideout room. One owner said they added the awning after ice accumulated on their slide's roof and prevented them from retracting the room.

Be sure you test drive the unit. There shouldn't be any wind whistle, rattles or creaking while you are traveling.

We wondered if the presence of the slideout's wall behind the driver's seat would be a distraction. I wasn't even aware of the wall being there when I drove. Two letter writers agreed.

Vicki: We spoke with owners who specifically chose RVs that were functional with the room retracted. They wanted to be sure they could stay in those few RV parks that couldn't accommodate slideout rigs. We discovered there were times when it would have been inconvenient to extend the slide. The ability to live comfortably with the slide retracted was something we appreciated in our test unit.

We stayed in commercial RV parks while we were traveling in our slideout. There were no problems finding campsites wide enough. At first though, we had to remind ourselves to park further to the right in the campsite than we were accustomed to.

When children were around, we were more comfortable if one of us stood outside as a "spotter" while the room was extended or retracted.

A couple of owners mentioned that it took more time for the heater and air conditioners to warm up and cool down the interior. We discovered that the insulation on the walls and floors of some slideout rooms was less than in the rest of the coach.

Several people commented on how much they like the slides that provide openable windows at each end of the slideout room. I know we enjoyed the light airy feeling afforded by these windows.

Nobody mentioned having any difficulty with the two-inch difference between the levels of the coach and slideout floors. The front edge of the couch and the ends of the bench-seat dinette in our borrowed motorhome were flush with the edge of the slideout floor and presented no problems. We have seen a couple of table and chair arrangements, however, where dining room chairs perched precariously close to the floor's drop-off.

We have also seen a number of RVs where the difference in floor levels in front of the couch bordered on being a hazard.

One manufacturer has a slide whose floor drops flush with the coach floor. I'm sure other manufacturers will soon follow suit.

Most of the slideout owners acknowledged they had sacrificed interior and exterior cabinet space but felt the extra elbow room was worth it.

We, along with others, noticed a slight decrease in fuel mileage with the slideout units. All of us, however, were in longer rigs. It is difficult to say how much of the decrease was due to the added weight of the room and how much was attributable to the heavier weight of the bigger RV.

It seems reasonable to assume, though, that an identical RV without the slideout room would have more cargo carrying capacity and possibly get better fuel mileage.

Pay particularly close attention to the slide's drive mechanism. If the drive system gets out of adjustment it can cause damage.

We kept track with our test vehicle. Between normal use and demonstrations for the curious, the slideout room was extended and retracted 28 times in a two-week period. The mechanism worked flawlessly every time.

Unfortunately, mechanical things do break down. Ask the salesperson to demonstrate how the room is manually retracted if the mechanism fails to operate for some reason.

One owner, who observed the slide's hydraulic hoses passing through a storage compartment, expressed concern about the possibility of leaking hydraulic fluid.

Another wrote "I will never have another RV without a slide (even if I experience difficulties later)". And another said they are looking forward to multiple slides on their next RV.

Joe: Vicki and I are contrarians. It is not unusual for us to head south when others drive north. So don't be shocked when we tell you we prefer not to have a slideout model. The extra aisle space just isn't important to us.

We are extended RV travelers. We generally travel two to three hundred miles a day, rarely stay in one place longer than two or three days and are on the road for two to three months at a time.

Setting up camp, for us, means parking, leveling, and connecting only those hookups we absolutely need. Getting ready to travel involves nothing more than disconnecting the hookups and starting the engine. The interior of our RV is always ready to travel.

Minimal campground setup, lots of convenient storage space and maximum cargo-carrying capacity are more important to us than extra aisle space.

We missed the deep cabinets over the couch and dinette. (By the way, we prefer a bench seat dinette because it provides storage under the seats and can double as a guest bed.) We also left a lot of "stuff" behind in our 32-foot motorhome's exterior bays that wouldn't fit in the bays of the 37-foot slideout.

Vicki didn't appreciate how much she uses the kitchen table during meal preparation until the slideout moved the table away from the kitchen counter.

Besides, like you, we have neglected to secure the refrigerator door and have had RVers wave us down to remind us we had forgotten to raise the entry step or lower the TV antenna. I don't know if I could handle someone reminding me we had forgotten to retract the slideout.

Do your homework. Compare the various makes and models. Ask owners of slideouts what they would look for in their next RV. Judging by the letters we received, there is minimal downside to a slideout and once you have experienced the added space you'll never want to do without one.

Switching From Gas To Diesel

"What's it like to switch from a gasoline-powered RV to a diesel for the first time? What's the difference between operating and driving a diesel as opposed to a gas vehicle? Do you really have to understand all that techno-jargon to be a successful diesel RVer?"

Joe: We didn't know the answers to your questions. Vicki and I had never operated any kind of diesel-powered vehicle. Nobody can ever accuse us of being technical experts. Who, we asked, would be better qualified to find out?

Our evaluation unit was a 37-foot, diesel-pusher motorhome. It was powered by a Cummins 230 horsepower, 5.9 liter, turbo-charged engine. This is the diesel engine that is most often compared to the big-block gasoline-powered engines when experts discuss gas versus diesel.

Vicki: We spent three hours with a "walk through" expert employed by a local dealer who specializes in selling diesel-powered motorhomes.

When I turned the ignition key to start the engine, a buzzer screamed at me. "This motorhome is equipped with air brakes." the walk-through specialist explained. "That's the low air-pressure warning. Watch the air-pressure gauge. When it reaches 60 pounds per square inch the buzzer will stop and the transmission will allow you to go into gear."

It took a minute or so before the buzzer finally shut itself off. "Now flip that lever to fill the suspension system's air-bags" he directed. Silently and almost imperceptibly the motorhome rose a couple of inches.

The brake pedal was hinged at the floor and resembled an accelerator pedal. It took a few practice touches before I stopped throwing everyone into their seat belts. Air brakes are sensitive.

I pushed the accelerator to the floor as we entered a freeway. There wasn't a neck-snapping jolt but the motorhome moved out smartly. We merged into the freeway traffic at 55 miles per hour.

When decelerating on level roads, the diesel engine seemed to slow the motorhome almost as well as the gasoline engines in other motorhomes I had driven.

Just before reaching the freeway off ramp, I switched on the exhaust brake. When I lifted my foot from the accelerator, it felt as if I had thrown out an anchor. The engine, assisted by the transmission automatically shifting to a lower gear, really pulled the speed down. Wow!

By the time we had driven six blocks through stop and go traffic, I was touching the brakes like a pro. Air pressure remained constant in spite of the repeated use of the brake pedal.

Once the parking brake was set, I flipped the air-dump switch to deflate the suspension air bags. With a sigh the motorhome sank closer to the ground.

We learned that the engine oil, transmission fluid and coolant levels could all be checked by opening an outside compartment at the rear of the motorhome.

An air cleaner indicator was also located in this compartment. This gadget lets you know when it's time to change the air filter. A diesel engine consumes a lot of air, so it's important that the airway remains unrestricted.

Finally, we were introduced to the fuel-water separator. Here, water and sediment are separated from the fuel and settle into the bottom of a transparent bowl. A drain valve at the bottom of the bowl allows you to drain any accumulated water or sediment. The manual suggests this be done every driving day.

I made sure that Joe was paying close attention to these last few details.

Joe: We spent the months of January, February and March traveling and living in that diesel motorhome with a small car in tow. Our coast to coast route took us across mountains and desert. Temperatures ranged from 20 to 95 degrees. One year ago, we had taken the same route with identical conditions in a 36-foot gasoline-powered motorhome. It was a fair comparison of the two power plants.

Driving the diesel wasn't much different than driving a gasoline rig. Put it in gear, step on the accelerator and go. Acceleration was a little bit slower in the diesel. Hill climbing speed was about the same. Our impression was that while the gasoline-powered motorhome moved across the country satisfactorily, the diesel rig accomplished it effortlessly.

The exhaust brake took all the thrill out of driving down a long, steep hill. On one 12-mile, six-percent downgrade (with our car in tow) I only touched the airbrakes twice.

The diesel's fuel consumption was a consistent 10 miles per gallon. Last year's gasoline rig got between 6 and 7 miles per gallon.

The diesel's preventive maintenance costs are higher than the gasoline rig's. One of our local RV dealerships charges $185 to change a diesel's oil and oil filter versus $54 for a gasoline motorhome. Changing a diesel's air and fuel filters would run an additional $200 as opposed to $60 for a gasoline rig.

When we summed up the overall cost of fuel, oil and filter changes, the cost per mile was about the same for both rigs.

We learned that a diesel owner must pay particular attention to the quality of fuel that goes into the RV's tank.

Water can get into diesel fuel from the condensation that results when a fuel station's storage tanks sit partially empty for long periods of time

The presence of water in diesel fuel can corrode vital engine parts. It also permits the growth of micro-organisms in the fuel. This slimy fungus will eventually clog the fuel filter and, if not destroyed, make its way into the fuel injector pump and injectors. You don't want that to happen.

Neither do the commercial truckers. They can't afford, nor would they tolerate, getting a tank of bad fuel. It only made sense, then, to get our fuel at a reputable, busy truck stop.

We discovered a number of truck stops that had RV fuel islands. More and more truck stops are welcoming RV drivers. Check them out.

Diesel fuel is susceptible to cold weather. When temperatures drop into the low teens, the fuel begins to thicken. To help prevent this, refiners blend and winterize their fuel according to the location of the country and its expected temperatures.

We refueled every two to three hundred miles with fuel that had been blended for that area's expected temperatures. Even though outside temperatures dropped to 20 degrees, we experienced no problems.

Going to high volume truck stops also assured us we weren't buying last summer's fuel.

Vicki: We made a couple of other observations about the difference in having a diesel RV.

Leaving a campground quickly and quietly in the pre-dawn hours was no longer an option with the diesel. If the roar of the required three minute engine warm up didn't wake up our neighbors, the scream of the air-pressure warning buzzer did.

I appreciated the fact that the rear pusher design removed the engine noise from the driver's compartment. Conversation could be held in a normal tone of voice.

That and the way the diesel chassis' air-bag suspension system seemed to float the motorhome over the highway made me a convert.

What's it like to switch from a gasoline-powered RV to a diesel for the first time? It's exciting, interesting and easy to do.

What's the difference between operating and driving a diesel as opposed to a gasoline-powered RV? Not that much, actually. The diesel just seems to do the job with less effort.

Do you really have to understand all that techno-jargon to be a successful diesel RVer? We still don't. But the diesel owner should make a point of becoming familiar with the characteristics of diesel fuel and the importance of maintaining and protecting the diesel's fuel delivery system.

Operating and maintaining a diesel engine (just like a gasoline engine) takes a bit of knowledge and thought. But after you've done it for a while it becomes second nature. Just put it in gear, step on the accelerator and go.

About Diesel Fuel

Diesel engines, because they have fewer moving parts, enjoy a reputation of having fewer mechanical problems than gasoline engines. When they do have problems, though, chances are they will be fuel related.

If you are thinking about buying a diesel-powered RV, make a point of becoming familiar with the characteristics of diesel fuel and the importance of maintaining and protecting the diesel's fuel delivery system.

A good place to begin is the ratings and grades of the over-the-road diesel fuels available.

Owners of gasoline vehicles are accustomed to seeing the octane rating of the fuel they purchase. Diesel fuel's loose counterpart is called "cetane." Cetane is a measure of the fuel's ignition quality. The higher the rating, the faster the fuel will ignite.

Fuels with a cetane rating below 40 may cause hard starting, engine knock and poor mileage. Since nearly all diesel refined in the United States has a cetane rating of at least 40, you probably won't see a selection of cetane ratings on diesel pumps.

You may, however, see two grades of diesel fuel available, 2D (Grade Number 2) and 1D (Grade Number 1).

2D is the grade most diesel engine manufacturers specify for optimum performance and the one you'll see available at most diesel pumps.

The good news about 2D diesel fuel is that its high paraffin content gives it a lot of power. The bad news is the paraffin begins to crystallize when temperatures drop into the teens.

The temperature reading when this crystallization begins to occur is known as the "cloud point." You can actually see the fuel get cloudy from the crystals.

At cloud point the paraffin wax crystals (along with ice crystals) begin to clog up the fuel filter and restrict the fuel flow. You don't want this to happen.

As the temperature continues to drop and reaches 10 degrees or less, the wax crystals thicken and prevent fuel flow altogether. The temperature reading when this occurs is referred to as the "pour point". You really don't want this to happen.

The good news about 1D diesel fuel is that its lower paraffin content means its "cloud point" and "pour point" are not reached until much lower temperatures. The bad news is that its lower paraffin content means it has less power than 2D diesel fuel.

To deal with the effects of cold weather, the refiners winterize their fuels with additives or by blending 1D fuel with 2D fuel. The fuel is winterized or blended according to the location of the country and its expected temperatures. The lower the expected temperatures, the lower the "cloud point" of the fuel shipped to that area.

During cold weather, diesel pumps may be posted with either the cloud point or the pour point of the fuel. Cloud point temperature is more important because that is when the fuel will start clogging the filter.

Cross country RV travelers should keep in mind that if they get caught in a Colorado mountain freeze with diesel fuel purchased at a New Mexico desert truck stop, they could conceivably end up with a tank full of gelatin.

One way to avoid this is to top off your fuel tank every two to three hundred miles with fuel blended for that region's expected temperature. Be sure you go to a busy fuel station. You don't want to take on a tank of last summer's fuel.

Before you put your diesel rig into storage, think about what the temperatures will be when you take it out. It only makes sense to fill the tank with the type of fuel that will start and run your engine when you take it out of storage.

One of the biggest concerns for diesel owners should be the presence of water in their fuel. Diesel engines depend upon their fuel to lubricate and cool tiny engine parts. Water that gets past the filters and into the engine displaces that fuel. Water that remains in the tank promotes rust. It also permits the formation of ice crystals in winter and bacterial growth during the summer.

The most common way that water gets into the fuel is condensation. Condensation takes place when moisture laden air condenses on the cool inner walls of a refinery's storage tanks, a fuel station's storage tanks or your own RV's fuel tank. The emptier the tank, the more surface available for condensation. The more humid the air, the more moisture available for condensation. The longer the condition exists, the more water there will be in the fuel.

Water is heavier than diesel fuel. It will settle to the bottom of the storage or fuel tank.

Where the water and diesel fuel interface, bacteria (live micro-organisms) can thrive. Left unchecked, this slimy fungus can coat the walls of your fuel tank and fuel lines, clog your filters and injectors and bring your vacation plans to a slimy halt.

If you discover signs of a buildup of micro-organisms in your fuel, a fungicide, formulated for diesel fuel can be added to the fuel tank. As the bacteria dies, it will show up in the filters, so change your filters more often if you treat your fuel with fungicide.

Preventing water related problems is easier than curing them. Get your fuel at a high volume fuel station. Storage tanks that are filled frequently present the least opportunity for condensation. The rapid turnover of fuel also helps keep water and bacteria to a minimum.

Top off the fuel tank if your rig is going to sit in an RV park or storage yard for a while. This will minimize the amount of fuel tank surface available for condensation.

Drain any accumulated water or sediment from the fuel-water separator every travel day. Most of today's diesel engines come equipped with a fuel-water separator.

Water and sediment are separated from the fuel and settle into the bottom of a transparent bowl. A drain valve at the bottom of the bowl allows you to drain any accumulated water or sediment. If your rig doesn't already have a fuel-water separator, install one.

Some rigs come equipped with a drain in the bottom of the fuel tank. If it's possible, drain the water from the bottom of the fuel tank once in a while.

Good, clean fuel is vital to a diesel's performance. You don't want to get a bad tank of fuel. Neither do the commercial truckers. Do what the truckers do; get your fuel at a reputable, high-volume truck stop.

A number of truck stops welcome RV business. Most of them identify themselves as travel plazas. Check them out.

Now that you know why, it will be easy to follow these few simple guidelines for the care and fueling of your diesel RV:

>Use fuel produced by a reputable refiner.
>Buy at a high volume fuel station.
>Drain the water separator every travel day.
>Inspect the filter bowl for unusual sediment, clouding or fungus.

Change the filters according to the engine manufacturer's recommendations.
Top off your fuel tank before putting it into storage.

Owning and operating a diesel RV is different but it isn't difficult. Pay particular attention to the quality of fuel that goes into the RV's tank and to the proper maintenance of its fuel delivery system. You'll keep your engine troubles, if any, to a minimum.

Choosing A Tow Vehicle

"How do I go about choosing a tow vehicle to pull a travel trailer? Should I choose the tow vehicle first and then find a trailer it can tow? Or should I first select the trailer and then find a tow vehicle that can pull it? How do I determine whether the tow vehicle will be able to handle the trailer?"

Joe: The first thing you should do is identify (but not purchase) the trailer that best suits your RVing interests and needs.

Next, you should locate (but not purchase) the tow vehicle that can best handle the size and weight of that trailer. Once again, rely on the manufacturer's printed information to be sure the tow vehicle, its drive train and suspension are more than capable of towing the trailer you have in mind.

Finally, research to determine the best type of hitch for that trailer and tow vehicle combination.

In the best of all worlds, the tow vehicle will also satisfy your everyday transportation needs both while you are traveling and in between RV trips while you are home. In the real world, don't be surprised if you have to make a number of compromises.

Once these objectives are met, all you have to do is figure out how to pay for them.

Vicki: Here are a few guidelines for choosing a tow vehicle:

Decide whether a sedan, station wagon, van or pickup truck will best suit both your personal and towing needs.

Visit the dealership selling that vehicle and obtain a copy of the manufacturer's trailering guide and towing recommendations.

The towing recommendations will be expressed in weight, so do your homework and ascertain the following:

The *tow vehicle's* Gross Vehicle Weight Rating (GVWR). That's the maximum weight, including passengers (at 150 pounds each), fuel, cargo (including the trailer's hitch weight) and the weight of the tow vehicle itself, that the tow vehicle can safely carry down the road.

The *trailer's* Gross Vehicle Weight Rating (GVWR). That's the maximum weight, including water and propane, optional equipment, cargo, accessories and the weight of the trailer itself, that the trailer can safely carry down the road.

The *tow vehicle's* Gross Combined Weight Rating (GCWR). That's the maximum total weight of the fully loaded tow vehicle and fully loaded trailer that the tow vehicle may safely handle.

The *tow vehicle's* Trailer Weight Rating. That's the maximum trailer weight the manufacturer has determined the tow vehicle may tow.

It's not out of line to assume you will load your tow vehicle to its GVWR and pull a trailer also loaded to its GVWR. If the combined weight of the two vehicles exceeds the tow vehicle's Gross Combined Weight Rating, you need to lighten the load or get a tow vehicle with a higher Gross Combined Weight Rating.

Here's another way of looking at it. Place the fully loaded trailer and fully loaded tow vehicle on a scale. The total weight of both vehicles should not exceed the tow vehicle's Gross Combined Weight Rating.

If the trailer's fully loaded weight exceeds the tow vehicle's Trailer Weight Rating, you need to lighten the trailer weight or get a tow vehicle with a higher Trailer Weight Rating.

Joe: Not enough can be said about the importance of staying well within the manufacturer's weight limitations (for both the trailer and tow vehicle). Personally, I'd feel better knowing my tow vehicle was rated to handle at least ten percent more weight than I was towing.

Choose and equip your tow vehicle so it is more than adequate to do the job. Most manufacturers offer an optional towing package. It costs less to order the package than to add the equipment after you take delivery.

When it comes to choosing between adequate power and fuel economy, I would take the power. I've never seen an RVer drive to the top of a long, steep grade, get out of his rig, kick the tires and curse his RV for having too much power.

Before you buy your RVing combination be sure the manufacturers of the tow vehicle, trailer and hitch all agree you have a towing combination that is made for each other.

Do your homework, pay attention to the manufacturer's written recommendations, allow some margin for safety and be sure the tow vehicle you choose will take you where you want to go and let you do the things you want to do.

Dinghy Towing

"I am considering buying a Class A motorhome and towing a small car. I've seen motorhomes towing cars with all four wheels on the ground, on a dolly, and on a trailer. What are the advantages and disadvantages of each method? I asked this while camping last summer but the discussion generated more heat than light."

Joe: Think about how often you will be towing and how frequently you'll be hitching up and unhitching the car.

Towing a car with all four wheels on the ground is probably the easiest and most convenient method. It also appears to be the most popular. This might be your best choice if you're going to tow often and unhitch frequently.

First, be sure you check with the manufacturer of your car to determine if it is designed to be towed with all four wheels on the ground.

The transmissions of many vehicles equipped with front-wheel drive and/or automatic transmissions can be damaged if they are towed with the drive wheels on the ground.

If that is the case with your car, aftermarket products are available that allow vehicles with front-wheel drive and/or automatic transmissions to be towed without affecting the transmission.

Transmission lubrication pumps are available that will lubricate the transmission while the vehicle is being towed. Lockout devices can be added to the drive wheels of some front-wheel drive vehicles allowing them to free wheel.

Transmission "uncouplers" can be installed on rear-wheel drive vehicles to separate the drive shaft from the transmission.

Our rear-wheel drive car is equipped with a transmission "uncoupler". Moving a lever in the driver's compartment disconnects the driveshaft from the automatic transmission before we tow. A quick move of the lever reconnects the two when we arrive at our destination.

We have towed the car about seventy thousand miles and driven it an additional ninety thousand. The disconnect mechanism has performed flawlessly.

Have a professional hitch shop mount a baseplate for the towbar on the front of the car. The same shop should also be able to wire the car's brake and tail lights so they will operate in sync with the motorhome's lights.

Detachable light bars (with brake and tail lights) can be used if you don't want to mess with the car's wiring. They're not as convenient, but they'll do the job.

Check with the manufacturer of your motorhome to determine if its brakes are adequate to stop the additional weight of your towed vehicle. If not, you should consider one of the many products that will activate your car's brakes when you apply the motorhome's brakes.

The hitching procedure is usually pretty simple. Aligning the car's towbar with the motorhome's hitchball usually involves one person directing while another drives the car. However, with a little practice, a person can learn to accomplish this task alone. Telescoping and self-adjusting towbars are also available to make this an easy one-person operation.

Once the car is hooked up, the ignition key is turned to a position that releases the steering wheel lock. This allows the car's front wheels to turn left or right while going around corners.

It should be noted that you shouldn't back up when towing a car with all four wheels on the ground. The car's front wheels will cramp to the left or right. This could damage the car's steering and alignment mechanisms.

Towing a car with a dolly has a couple of advantages. The car itself requires no special equipment, and the dolly can be equipped with its own brakes.

The hitching procedure with a dolly can be a little more involved and time consuming than the "four wheels on the ground" method.

First, the dolly has to be hitched to the motorhome, the drive wheels of the car are driven up on the dolly, and the car is secured to the dolly.

A light bar with brake and tail lights is then mounted on the car. If the car is a front-wheel drive model and you don't want to bother with a light bar, the car's tail and brake lights can be wired to operate in sync with the motorhome's.

Keep in mind that the dolly will add to the gross combined weight of the towing unit and that most dollies are not designed to be backed with a car on board.

There is also the minor consideration of what to do with the dolly at the campground.

Towing a car on a trailer offers the advantages of having brakes on the trailer and the ability to back the trailer. If the trailer is enclosed, the car can be protected from the dirt and the elements

It's a bit of a bother, however, deciding what to do with the trailer once you've reached your destination. Not many campsites are large enough to accommodate a motorhome, a trailer and a car.

Be sure the hitch weight of the trailer doesn't exceed the motorhome's limitations. Don't forget to add the trailer's hitch weight to the motorhome's gross vehicle weight. The trailer will also add to the gross combined weight of the towing combination.

If you're considering buying a vehicle that you intend to tow behind a motorhome, I'd recommend you look for one whose transmission is compatible with towing, whose front end will easily accept a towbar's baseplate and whose brake and tail light wiring can be easily connected to your motorhome's.

Microwave/Convection Ovens

"My husband and I are looking for our third RV. Our other RVs had propane ovens and I felt comfortable cooking in them. It seems like so many of the new RVs have combination microwave/convection ovens instead of propane ovens. Is it hard to get used to a convection oven, and will I be happy with the results?"

Vicki: Until the last few years, standard equipment for most RVs was a three or four burner range and a propane oven. Today, a lot of RVs come equipped with a combination microwave/convection oven above the range and offer the propane oven as an option.

I enjoy cooking and do a lot of it when we're in our RV. An oven has always been important to me. I asked a sales person why the propane ovens were no longer standard. He said that since a microwave/convection oven could do anything a propane oven could do, the propane oven wasn't needed.

Now, a microwave/convection oven requires household (120 volt) electricity to operate. We do a lot of dry camping where electrical hookups are not available. We can use our generator to operate the microwave but there are times when we prefer not to disturb our neighbors or the serenity of a campground with the roar and exhaust of a generator. The propane oven can be used whether we have hookups or not. I thought a propane oven was still a necessity for us.

Recently, though, we had the opportunity to spend three months in a motorhome equipped with a combination microwave/convection oven. My adjustment to the "new fangled contraption" was painless and effortless. In fact, I became a real convert.

When using the microwave alone, it was the same as any other microwave oven. If the convection was used alone, it was much the same as using my electric oven at home. It cooked cleanly and evenly (no burned bottom on the biscuits as we've had in our propane ovens).

Now for the best part. The microwave and convection features can be used simultaneously. It's called "mixed bake". The microwave cooks the inside while the convection cooks and browns the outside. What a time saver. Our favorite recipes cooked in about two-thirds to three-quarters of the time.

During that trip we either had an electric hookup or we could use our generator if necessary. The motorhome was also equipped with a 2,000 watt inverter. It could convert battery power to household electricity and operate the microwave. I never missed the propane oven.

Think about what type of camping facilities you usually stay in and how much cooking you plan to do.

You may want to stick with the propane oven if you prefer dry camping in government campgrounds. Operating the microwave via an inverter does consume battery power.

On the other hand, if you typically spend most of your time in campgrounds that provide electric hookups, you'll probably enjoy having the convection oven.

Our next RV will definitely have a combination microwave/convection oven. I think I'll forego the propane oven and take the cupboard or drawers that comes in its place.

When we do not have access to household electricity to run the microwave/convection oven, I will simply prepare a meal that can be fixed on the range, or maybe I'll just make ...dinner reservations.

Clothes Washer/Dryers

"My husband and I will be buying a larger RV within the next few months. We plan on spending long periods of time on the road. I can't decide whether or not to get a washer and dryer. Do you have one in your RV?"

Vicki: When we bought our last RV, I agonized over whether or not to get a washer and dryer. I talked to a number of people who had combination washer/dryers in their RVs. They all pointed out that while the capacities were small and the drying cycle took a long time, it was worth the slight inconvenience to avoid being dependent on laundromats.

At that time, I opted to have the large storage cupboard instead of the washer/dryer that would have occupied that space. The biggest factor in my decision was that since I would need electric, water and sewer hookups to operate the washer/dryer, I would probably be in a campground that also had a laundry room.

Not long after that, we did a livability evaluation on a 37-foot motorhome. Our evaluation unit had a combination washer/dryer, so I took the opportunity to learn and experiment.

Here's what I found: The washer/dryer has about one-third the capacity of our washer and dryer at home.

It's possible to operate it without a water and sewer hookup (be sure to watch the water and holding tank levels closely), but we recommend full RV hookups. According to the manufacturer, the wash cycle consumes anywhere from 12 to 16 gallons of water and, believe it or not, the drying cycle uses another 3 gallons.

The wash cycle, depending on the setting, took from 30 to 45 minutes and consistently did a great job.

The drying cycle, depending on the setting and the type of clothing, took anywhere from one to three hours. Heavy towels and jeans seemed to take forever to dry.

I came to the conclusion that doing one load of laundry every day would keep dirty clothes to a minimum. I generally started the washer after dinner because the RV's electrical system prevented me from operating the microwave and the washer/dryer at the same time.

I found myself using the washer/dryer more and more for delicate and light articles of clothing. It was especially handy if I only had a few articles of the same color that required a separate load. I continued to use campground laundry rooms and commercial laundromats for towels, sheets, jeans and other heavy articles.

Do I want a washer/dryer in my next RV? It depends. If the RV we choose has the washer/dryer in it, I will happily use it. However, if I have to consciously choose between a big storage cupboard and an expensive optional washer/dryer, I'll probably continue looking for campgrounds with nice laundry rooms.

(Note: After a two year search, we recently bought a 36-foot motorhome for our extended RV travels. It came equipped with a washer/dryer. I love it!)

What To Take

"My husband and I are getting ready to go on an extended trip in our RV. I'm accustomed to packing the RV for weekends, but I'm not sure what I'll need to take for three months. I'm afraid I'll take too much. And, what kinds of kitchen appliances and household items do folks use in their RVs?"

Joe: Try to visualize the places you'll be going and the things you'll be doing. Will the weather be hot or cold; wet or dry? How dressed up will you need to be? How often will you be preparing meals in your RV?

The kitchen utensils and appliances you take with you will depend not only on the amount of storage space you have but also on how much cooking you do. We know folks who never use their RV kitchens at all. They eat all of their meals in restaurants. Most of the extended RV travelers that we've met, however, seem inclined to cook in their RVs just as they would at home. You can eat convenience foods for just so long.

During the summer we use our portable barbecue for many of our meals. Cooking outside is one way to keep the inside of the RV cool. During pleasant weather, a barbecue, combined with the range in the RV and a microwave/convection oven seem to satisfy all our meal preparation needs.

During the winter our favorite kitchen appliance is the crockpot. Stepping into a warm RV, the aroma of dinner cooking in a crockpot can be a real treat on a cold winter day.

Once in awhile, with our generator providing the power, we cook in the crockpot while we're traveling down the road. Properly timed, dinner is ready when we arrive at our destination.

Vicki: Another favorite appliance is our pressure cooker. We bought it at an RV show a couple of years ago. It's fast and convenient and is really handy when we're in a hurry.

Rather than a drip coffee maker, we prefer an "old fashioned" electric percolator. Since it is made of stainless steel rather than glass, it's easy to store and we don't have to worry about the glass carafe breaking.

We also use a toaster on a regular basis and, occasionally, an electric mixer.

Our next appliance purchase for the RV will be an electric skillet. It will come in handy to use outside when I'm preparing something messy or when the range's three burners are not enough

Toaster ovens are a versatile appliance that some RVers just would not be without. They can accomplish a variety of baking and heating chores. And, along with portable barbecues, portable stoves and electric skillets, they allow cooking to be done outside on hot summer days.

Some of the kitchen appliances that we've heard others say they can't live without are blenders, waffle makers and bread machines. Can you imagine traveling down the road with the aroma of baking bread filling your rig? It's certainly possible if you have a motorhome equipped with a generator; but, do you have the storage space for such a large appliance?

When it comes to clothing, take enough to last seven to ten days and plan on doing laundry once a week. Keep in mind that mix-and-match outfits will help to minimize the amount of clothes you need. Take durable clothing. Commercial washers and dryers can be hard on clothes.

Make sure you take clothing for all kinds of weather. Even if you are convinced that the weather will be warm, take a couple of sweatshirts and a jacket. During our first winter trip to Florida we took only warm-weather clothes. It turned out to be one of the coldest winters in the state's history.

We always have rain gear (including umbrellas) available. You never know when a storm may appear. Joe keeps a pair of slip-on rain boots in our RV. Not only are they handy for going out in the rain, he also uses them when washing the RV or when it's necessary to troop through wet grass or mud to get to the utility connections.

Most RVers dress pretty casually, but it's a good idea to take one dressy outfit for each of you. You'll have a lot more flexibility in choosing restaurants and you never know when a "dressy" occasion may present itself.

We learned about dressy outfits the hard way during a visit with relatives in New England. When we arrived, we found that a family wedding was scheduled to take place. It was our big opportunity to see everybody at one time but we had only brought casual clothes. We had to go out and buy complete new outfits.

Put your dressy outfits in plastic dry-cleaning bags or garment bags and hang them at the back of the closet. Make sure that you also take all the accessories you'll need. Jewelry can be put with shoes and stuck in a corner of a closet or drawer. You may never use these clothes, but at least you will be prepared.

Joe: Equip your RV as completely as possible. Your RV should have its own linens, dishes, cooking utensils, small appliances and other items. This will minimize the amount stuff you have to load and unload before and after your RV trips. If things are permanently stored in the RV, it's unlikely they'll be left behind.

Personal appliances we can't do without and that are permanently stored in our RV include an electric razor, hair dryer and curling iron.

You might want to equip your RV with a small amount of office supplies. This would include pens, pencils, paper, envelopes, postage stamps, ruler, stapler, paper clips and calculator.

Lots of RVers are taking their computers and printers on the road. Laptops take less space and make it easier to send and receive e-mail.

A laundry basket containing soap, bleach and fabric softener should occupy a permanent spot in your RV. If you have the space, add an ironing board and iron. The ironing board could be a table top model. We have discovered that many campgrounds are making ironing boards and irons available to their guests.

Find a spot to store a vacuum cleaner, then buy a vacuum cleaner that will fit into it.

If you are a list maker, list all the items that you think you should take with you. The list should only include the things are that <u>not</u> already stored in the RV. As you load the items into the RV, cross them off the list.

Once you are happy with your list, make several copies. That way, you won't have to make a new list each time you leave on a trip.

Obviously, the most important things on the list will be those items that are absolutely irreplaceable. Those items would include prescription medications, reading glasses, cash, credit cards, checkbook and address book.

Vicki: Don't forget to take things to do in your leisure time. Will you be fishing, golfing, hiking? You don't want to forget those golf clubs or that favorite fishing pole. Be sure your checklist includes a camera and plenty of film (film is usually more expensive when purchased on the road).

If you enjoy reading, take a supply of books and, of course, you can always buy more along the way. When either of us is finished reading a book or magazine, we either donate it to an RV park's exchange library or we leave it in the campground laundry room. Somehow, a book or magazine doesn't seem so expensive when you know it will be enjoyed by others.

Keep in mind that as long as you have the irreplaceable things with you, it's not a big deal if you forget anything else. You can always buy another along the way or you can do without.

Selecting Campgrounds

"We bought our motorhome two years ago. Since then we have only stayed in a couple of nearby campgrounds recommended by friends. This summer we want to spend three months touring the country. What criteria should we use when choosing a campground while traveling?"

Joe: It depends upon a number of factors: the amount of time you intend to stay in any one location, the type of facilities you want and, of course, your budget.

We suggest you take advantage of this travel opportunity to experiment with a variety of parks and campgrounds.

Begin by learning how to read your RV park and campground directory. The listings and information it contains will help you select the RV parks and campgrounds that best suit your needs.

You'll find RV park and campground directories at book and RV accessory stores. The directories list the RV parks and campgrounds by area. You simply open the book to the area where you want to stay to find the campgrounds available.

Each individual listing will include information about the campground, its facilities and fees. Owners of large rigs should pay particular attention to the campground's size limitations.

Commercial directories don't always list government campgrounds. Try to obtain listings or directories of the national, state, county and city campgrounds in the areas you are visiting.

Reservations at campgrounds and RV parks should be made according to the location and time of year just as you would at a hotel or motel. If you want to stay on a holiday or summer weekend, reservations might be wise. On the other hand, if you will arrive during the middle of the week or during the off season, reservations may not be necessary.

Many RV travelers prefer to travel without the constraints of an itinerary. They don't make reservations because they don't know where they will be on any given day. Others, with a particular destination and time frame in mind, will secure their campsite by making reservations. RVing offers this freedom of choice.

Generally speaking, RV parks and campgrounds fall into two basic categories; enroute and destination.

Enroute parks are those in which you only intend to spend a night or two while traveling.

When you just want to spend one night in a campground, easy access and convenient site setup will probably be more important than scenic surroundings. You'll also appreciate a campground or RV park that is conveniently close to the highway, yet far enough away to avoid the sounds of traffic.

With any luck the campground will have level, pull-through sites. That will save you the time and trouble of unhitching and leveling.

Will a simple park with basic amenities do the job? We have seen a growing number of no-frills overnight RV parks along the interstates.

Most offer level, pull-through sites with full hookups for as little as $10 a night. Showers and restrooms are usually small and laundry rooms typically nonexistent. Some may have playground equipment but rarely a pool. Personally, we find these RV parks offer everything we need for a quick overnight stay.

A destination campground or RV park is one where you intend to spend some time. It may be in a national park you wish to explore, on the outskirts of a big city you wish to visit or adjacent to a lake that needs fishing.

A lot of RVers will select a destination campground in a convenient, central location. This enables them to make exploratory day trips in different directions. We call this "hub-and-spoke" camping.

When you intend to stay at a destination campground for a few days or longer, the size, orientation and surroundings of your site may be more important to you than the time it takes to back, level and hook up to utilities.

Vicki: Consider the availability and convenience of utility hookups, laundry room and other facilities when selecting either an enroute park or destination campground.

Before registering at the campground office, you may want to inspect the facilities that are important to you and your family. I make a point of checking the number and cleanliness of the campground's washers and dryers if I plan on doing laundry while we are there.

Be sure to check the availability of the swimming pool if your kids are looking forward to a swim. The only thing more disappointing than a drained swimming pool is one that is full of water but off limits to kids.

And, speaking of kids, some RV parks are "adult only" but fail to publicize the fact. Read your campground directory listings and their accompanying advertisements carefully. Look for clues that may indicate an "adult only" park. Call ahead if you have any doubts.

We have heard complaints from 50-year-olds about RV resorts with a 55 and older policy. Some parks, on the other hand, make it very clear in their advertising they welcome kids under 55 years of age.

Joe: How much do you want to pay? You get what you pay for; or so they tell me. RV resorts usually cost more than the average RV park. Government campgrounds generally cost less than commercial campgrounds.

Most RV parks and campgrounds post their campsite rates on a board behind the registration desk. There may be a basic overnight fee with additional charges for each hookup service. There may also be additional charges for more than two persons, pets, additional vehicles and use of air conditioners or electric heaters.

Some RVers want full hookups every night and are willing to pay for them, others may only request electric and water hookups. They will use the campground's disposal station when they leave in the morning.

Before you register, ask about discounts. Members of RV clubs like Good Sam, Escapees and FMCA frequently qualify for discounts of ten percent or more at many RV parks and campgrounds (this includes some government campgrounds).

Ask about weekly rates. On more than one occasion we have found the weekly rate cheaper than what the daily rate would have been for the five or six days we actually stayed.

While you are registering be sure to ask for:

A pull-through site if you have a long rig.

A site wide enough to accommodate your slide-out room(s).

Hookup connections on the left (driver's) side of the campsite. (That's where your RV's connections are located.)

A shady site in the summer (bird and tree sap droppings may come with it).

A sunny site when it's cold.

A site close to the recreational facilities if you won't mind the noise.

A site convenient to the restroom if you won't mind the foot traffic.

A site near the laundry room if you are going to use it.

We've talked to RVers who prefer the consistent quality and facilities of chain campgrounds like KOA. Others insist the RV parks have a campground directory rating of 7/7/7 or higher and some stick to membership campgrounds.

Vicki and I, on the other hand, like to adventurize. It's not unusual for us to impulsively pull into a park we know nothing about. We've had a few disappointments but we've also discovered a lot of wonderful RV parks and campgrounds around the country.

Experiment. Spend a few days in an RV resort that offers a golf course, tennis courts and organized recreation activities. Dry camp in a government campground. Stay in a variety of commercial RV parks and campgrounds with different ratings and facilities. It won't be long before you develop your own campground selection criteria.

Locating Uncrowded Campgrounds

"We are relatively new to RVing. We often see articles about RV camping in the boonies or see pictures of RVers at some remote body of water. Is this reality? How do you find remote, pristine wilderness to dry camp in while traveling? What other options do we have besides using campgrounds, rest areas or truck stops?"

Joe: We have dry camped on isolated beaches along the Baja Peninsula, on a secluded section of lakefront in central California, on open stretches of desert in Arizona, next to a glacier in Alaska and on a lonely bluff overlooking the coast in Maine. So, yes, it is a reality. But, in all cases, we just happened upon them. In fact, some of our best camping experiences were the result of happenstance. We refer to those occasions as serendipity.

Vicki: You'll find remote dry camping opportunities available on government land administered by the National Park Service, National Forest Service, Bureau of Land Management and the U.S. Army Corps of Engineers. All of these agencies will send maps and information to you.

Keep an eye open for fairgrounds, race tracks, city and county parks. Many of them offer camping or overnight opportunities. We have found camping facilities at wildlife refuges and on land controlled by lumber and power companies.

Joe: If you enjoy uncrowded campgrounds, be contrarians like Vicki and me. We prefer to travel during the off-season months of April, May, June, September and October.

When the snowbirds are heading south for the winter, we are enroute to New England for the fall colors. During holiday weekends when the destination campgrounds are packed, we spend our time in relatively uncrowded enroute parks.

Vicki: Build your own library of campground and RV park directories. You will find them at RV accessory stores. You'll find others are available from federal, state, and county governmental agencies, RV clubs, auto clubs and tourist bureaus.

We routinely stop at every state's welcome center. Most are located in rest areas just as you enter the state. You'll find maps and brochures describing places of interest and things to do. Ask the person behind the counter for directories to city, county and state campgrounds.

We have picked up some of the best leads to great camping spots while talking to fellow RVers in campground laundry rooms.

Joe and I have been RVing for over 30 years. We are still discovering new and exciting places to go and things to see and do. You are just beginning. Think of all the adventures that await you.

Self-Contained Camping

"We recently bought a 32-foot motorhome and have thoroughly enjoyed staying in RV parks with hookups. This fall we plan to visit a number of national parks where we will be camping self-contained for the first time. Do you have any advice that will make "roughing it" easier?"

Joe: You're going to discover that while most of the campgrounds in government parks may not offer utility hookups, they do have waste-water disposal stations and fresh-water faucets. "Roughing it" means the inconvenience of taking your RV to these facilities when it becomes necessary.

When you stay in most of today's commercial RV parks or campgrounds, chances are you enjoy the convenience of utility hookups. A water hose connects the RV's plumbing to the campground's water supply. An electric cord brings in campground power. A sewer hose empties the rig's waste into the campground's sewer system.

Hookups may even be available for cable TV and, if you're really lucky, there may be a telephone hookup. All the comforts of home while away from home.

Pull into a government campground, however, and you'll probably have to rely upon your rig's self-containment features.

Nearly all of today's RVs come equipped with self-containment features. An on-board storage tank carries fresh water. A "gray-water" holding tank captures waste water from the shower and sinks. A "black-water" holding tank collects toilet waste. One or more 12-volt batteries supply electrical power. A propane tank provides fuel for cooking, heating and to operate the refrigerator.

Self-containment capacities vary from rig to rig but most RVs will allow you to camp comfortably for at least two to three days without hookups.

Vicki: Seasoned RV campers have learned to extend their "dry camping" time by practicing conservation and expanding their RV's self-containment capabilities.

Here are some of their secrets for successful dry camping:

Conserve water. The less water you use, the fewer trips you'll have to make to the local water hydrant to refill your RV's water tank.

One obvious way to conserve the RV's fresh-water supply is to take advantage of the campground's restroom and shower facilities whenever possible.

If you do use your RV shower, take a "navy" shower. Use a minimal amount of water to get wet, turn off the water, soap yourself and then use only enough water to rinse off.

Don't let the water run while brushing your teeth or while washing your hands and face.

Use paper plates to reduce the number of dishes that have to be washed.

Wash dishes only once a day. Instead of pre-rinsing, use paper towels to wipe leftover food from the dishes.

Some RVers recycle dishwater by saving it (in a bucket or plastic jug) for flushing the toilet.

Minimizing the amount of water you consume means you'll also be conserving holding tank space.

There are not many RVs whose gray-water tanks equal the capacity of their fresh-water tanks. Since the sinks and showers drain into the gray-water tank, it's not unusual for some RVers to run out of gray-water holding-tank space long before they run out of fresh water.

Black-water tanks that capture toilet waste, however, are frequently larger than necessary.

With this in mind, one way you can save gray-water tank space is to wash dishes in a plastic dishpan and empty the dishwater into the toilet and its black-water tank. Some RVers even capture shower water and dump it into the black-water tank.

A covered waste-water collector, such as a Tote-Tank, can be connected to the RV's sewer outlet to capture gray water. Depending upon their size, Tote-Tanks can collect up to 30 gallons. They even have wheels that make it easier to take them to a campground's disposal station.

Joe: Conserve battery power. Most RVs come equipped with a Group 24 deep-cycle battery. This battery has a capacity of about 80 amp-hours of electricity.

A single 12-volt ceiling light bulb draws about 1.5 amps; a 9-inch color TV about 3 amps; and the furnace fan 7.5 amps while operating. Obviously, the less amps you consume, the longer your battery will last. So turn off unnecessary lights and keep 12 volt appliance operation to a minimum.

Check your 12-volt RV light fixtures. Many are equipped with two bulbs. Experiment to see if one bulb will do the job.

Consider replacing one or two 12-volt incandescent light fixtures with fluorescent ones. They consume less electricity and provide more light.

When it's time to replace the coach battery, buy a Group 27 deep-cycle battery. Its 105 amp-hour capacity is 30% greater than the Group 24's 80 amp-hours.

If one deep-cycle battery isn't sufficient for your needs, see if it's possible to install a second one. It's best to install two identical new batteries at the same time rather than simply connecting a new battery to your existing battery.

Check into the possibility of installing two 6-volt golf-cart batteries in your coach. Wired in series for a 12-volt output, the batteries will have a capacity of about 230 amp-hours.

A generator will provide 120-volt household power and slowly recharge your batteries.

If it won't disturb your neighbors, think about running your generator just after you get up in the morning and again around dinner time. This will allow you to take full advantage of all the electricity it produces. In addition to operating your lights, you'll probably be able to run the microwave, electric coffee pot, hair dryer, vacuum cleaner and other appliances.

Many RVers have installed solar systems in their RVs. The good news about solar power is, it really works. The bad news is, the equipment can be expensive. Do some research. A solar system could be a practical investment depending upon the amount of time you spend self-contained camping.

Vicki: Conserve propane. Keep in mind that the water heater and forced-air furnace are among the greatest consumers of propane.

Instead of allowing the water heater to cycle on and off all day, turn it on just once a day to heat water for showers and washing dishes. It takes only 30 to 40 minutes to heat the tank. Then you can turn it off for the remainder of the day.

If you only need enough hot water to do dishes, heat water in a tea kettle on the stove. That way you avoid turning on your water heater and heating six to ten gallons of water.

Better yet, fill up the kettle with hot water at the campground's restroom.

Another way to reduce propane consumption is by installing a catalytic heater. It uses considerably less propane than the other propane heaters and, unlike the fan of a forced air furnace, it doesn't use electricity.

Joe: When the RV's lights are dim, the water tank is empty and the holding tanks are full, you'll know it's time to move.

If the campground has a disposal station and a drinking water hydrant, "roughing it" will amount to moving your RV to the disposal station, dumping the waste water, refilling the fresh-water tank and returning to your campsite.

Or, you can move down the road and check into an RV park or a campground that offers electric, water and sewer hookups. The drive will probably recharge your batteries.

While there, you can refill your water tank, empty the holding tanks and take advantage of the 120-volt electricity to use your vacuum cleaner. Chances are they will also have a laundry room.

Experiment. Keep your eyes and ears open. You'll discover a number of ways to stretch your RV's self-containment capabilities.

Your RV can provide you with all the comforts of home while away from home. Take advantage of its versatility. Visit the government parks, stay in friends' long driveways and be sure to enjoy the full service facilities of the commercial RV parks and campgrounds.

The self-containment features of your RV are made to order for enjoying our government parks and campgrounds. You're heading for a great adventure!

Cold-Weather Camping

"We want to explore the mid-Atlantic states during January, February and March. Our travels will take us into freezing temperatures and light snow. How should we prepare our rig? Do you have any suggestions for winter camping?"

Joe: It's no secret to experienced RVers that cold weather months can be a great time to travel and camp in an RV. Traffic is lighter, campgrounds are uncrowded and the weather is stimulating.

Today's RVs are insulated, have efficient heating systems and provide a snug refuge from foul weather. Soup, coffee and hot chocolate are quickly prepared on the kitchen stove.

Comfort lovers can enjoy the luxury of curling up on the couch with a good book while others take advantage of outdoors activities. Clothing to match the changing weather is conveniently available in closets and drawers.

Prepare for the cold-weather season by draining and backflushing the engine's cooling system. Experts recommend a 50% water and 50% antifreeze mixture in the radiator to give you protection to 34 degrees below zero. This is also a good time to check the heater hoses and heater operation.

Engines demand more electrical starting power during cold weather. Check the battery's electrolyte level, clean the terminals and coat them with petroleum jelly.

Don't forget to lubricate the chassis and change the oil on your engine and generator. Check your owner's manual to see what grade of oil is recommended for the anticipated temperature range.

Check the condition of the windshield wiper blades and the operation of the windshield washer. Fill the reservoir with windshield washer fluid. By the way, windshield washer fluid contains methanol and won't freeze.

You'll want a set of tire chains if you think you'll encounter snow and ice. Practice putting them on while it's warm and dry.

Fill the propane tank. This will minimize condensation inside the tank and help prevent vaporization problems in cold temperatures.

Vicki: Your RV's built-in space heating system should be adequate for keeping the interior warm. Keep in mind, however, that a forced air furnace will not only consume propane but up to seven amps per hour of electricity as well. This could represent a considerable drain on the coach battery if no hookups are available.

You can reduce consumption of propane by augmenting the propane furnace with a portable electric heater. Be sure the RV hookup cord and any extension cord to the heater have a sufficient amperage rating to withstand the wattage of the heater. Divide the heater's maximum wattage by 120 (volts) to determine the minimum amperage rating of the electrical cord. (A 1,500 watt heater would require an electrical cord with a minimal rating of 12.5 amps.)

Many RVers who do a lot of self-contained camping use catalytic heaters. Catalytic heaters combine propane and oxygen over a platinum-impregnated pad. The chemical reaction releases energy in the form of radiated heat. It requires no electricity and utilizes propane more efficiently than a forced-air heater.

Most catalytic heaters are not vented to the outside. They consume oxygen from inside the RV and should only be operated when open windows can provide ventilation. A window and a roof vent, each open 18 square inches, should provide adequate ventilation for a 6,000 BTU catalytic heater.

Look for ways to improve your RV's ability to retain heat. You can block the cold radiated by a motorhome's windshield by hanging a heavy blanket between the driver's compartment and the rest of the coach.

Heavy drapes or curtains will insulate the coach windows against the cold. An insulating dead air space can be created by covering the inside of the windows with clear, heavy vinyl. Some RVers use sheets of Styrofoam to cover the interior of their windows.

Roof vents can be covered on the inside with Styrofoam or snap-on vinyl covers. Throw rugs, especially on vinyl flooring, will add insulation to the floors. They'll also protect the carpeting against tracked in dirt and moisture.

Weather-stripping around entry doors and exterior cabinet doors will prevent cold drafts.

Styrofoam or fiberglass insulation can be attached to the inside of exterior cabinet doors.

Joe: You'll want to examine your rig's plumbing to determine what measures may be needed to prevent damage from freezing temperatures.

The fresh-water tanks, water pump, pipes, drains, holding tanks and dumping valves of some RVs are protected by locating them in heated channels or compartments. The heat source is one or more ducts from the forced-air furnace. As long as the furnace runs periodically, the water in the pipes and tanks shouldn't freeze.

Other RVs, however, may have their drains, holding tanks and dumping valves below the floor and exposed to outside temperatures.

Empty the holding tanks if they will be subject to freezing and pour a couple of quarts of non-toxic, biodegradable antifreeze into each holding tank. This will protect the dump valves. Pour in more antifreeze as waste water fills the tanks. Pouring the antifreeze into the gray-water tank through the shower drain will also protect the drain pipe below the shower.

When outside temperatures approach freezing, disconnect, drain and store the drinking water and sewer-hookup hoses. Slightly opening the doors of interior cupboards that contain plumbing will allow heated air from the coach to circulate around the pipes.

Drain the water system if you are unable to protect the fresh-water pump or plumbing from freezing. Even better protection is provided by using compressed air to blow the remaining water from the pipes or by simply pumping non-toxic, potable antifreeze throughout the water system.

Some cold-weather RVers winterize and then don't use their plumbing system at all. Instead, they carry containers of drinking water inside the living area of the RV and rely completely upon the campground's restroom facilities. Call ahead to the campground if this is your plan. Some close their restrooms during the off season and others may only provide electrical hookups.

Vicki: You can use electric tank heating pads and electric heating tape to protect plumbing when you stay in a campground or RV park that provides electrical hookups.

We have used electric drop cords to protect plumbing in exterior cabinets. The heat from the lightbulb was sufficient to keep things from freezing.

Hot water and ordinary electric heating pads can be used for thawing out frozen hoses, pipes and valves. Our favorite tool is the hair dryer. We once used a hair dryer to melt ice from our TV antenna so it could be lowered for traveling.

Wherever you go during the fall and winter months be prepared for sudden drops in temperature. We were enroute to sunny Mexico one February and ran into freezing temperatures in Tucson, Arizona.

Before driving into an area on a dirt road, consider what it will be like to drive out on that road when it is slick from rain.

Try to camp in a spot that is open to the heat of the sun and, if possible, protected from the wind. You can minimize cold drafts by facing the RV into or away from the prevailing wind.

Keep in mind that snow accumulating on overhanging branches may eventually drop off in heavy clumps or perhaps bring down the brittle branches. Don't let snow block the refrigerator roof vent.

Cold-weather camping doesn't necessarily have to include freezing temperatures and snow, but be prepared for occasional rain and some cold weather. And don't be surprised if you find yourself in an almost empty campground experiencing warm, balmy weather.

Your RV is, in all likelihood, built for cold-weather camping. All you need to add is common sense and perhaps some antifreeze and snow chains. And don't forget the hot chocolate!

RVing On A Budget

"The idea of camping and traveling in an RV appeals to me but I am on a limited budget. What can I do to control the costs of RVing?"

Joe: That's a tough question. The answer depends on what you want to do in your RV. An RV, after all, simply provides mobile living accommodations for whatever activity you wish to pursue. Here are a few suggestions for controlling the costs of RVing:

You might consider buying a used, inexpensive rig. There are some great values in used RVs out there.

The least expensive way to get started in RVing may be to buy a used trailer that can be easily towed by your present transportation vehicle. You already have the tow vehicle. So your investment will be limited to the trailer, hitching equipment and mirrors.

Insurance and vehicle registration on an inexpensive used trailer will probably cost less than on a new one. Look for inexpensive camping equipment and RV furnishings at garage sales and thrift shops.

Go to the library. Check out the many books on choosing an RV. Shop for an RV by looking on RV dealers' lots and reading the classified section of the RV magazines and your local newspaper.

The most important thing to keep in mind when shopping for an RV is how, when and where you intend to use it. You don't have to invest a lot of money in an RV if you only intend to use it for a few weekend camping trips and an occasional two-week vacation.

Vicki: Shop for insurance. Talk to a number of insurance agents to find the best value of coverage for the premium.

Does the value of your RV warrant theft and collision insurance? If your RV is a trailer, will the tow vehicle's liability insurance cover you while you are on the road. Will your homeowner's policy offer you any protection while camping?

Check out the insurance company's reputation for responsiveness when their clients need them.

Joe: Learn how to do your own maintenance and minor repairs. Your RV's owner's manual should provide a maintenance schedule and may also offer instructions. You'll find RV repair and maintenance manuals at RV accessory stores and your local library.

Control your fuel costs. When selecting an RV, keep in mind that a lightweight rig won't consume as much fuel as the heavier ones.

You only use fuel when you're traveling. Look for campgrounds, attractions and activities that are located relatively close to home. You'll spend less money on fuel, less time on the road and have more time to enjoy your destination.

Vicki: Stay in affordable campgrounds. Study your campground and RV park directory. It gives you the tools you need to select an RV park or campground that offers the location, facilities and rates that will best satisfy your interests and budget. (We are writing this while parked in a clean, pleasant, no-frills, campground. Our site, with electric, water and sewer connections is only $15 a night.)

Many campgrounds, in addition to a basic nightly rate, charge an optional amount for electric, water, sewer, cable and telephone connections. You can control overnight costs by only taking (and paying for) the hookups you need.

Another way to control overnight costs is to take advantage of the discounts offered by campgrounds to members of RV clubs, AAA, AARP and other groups.

Ask the campground about weekly and monthly rates. Keep in mind that rates are cheaper in some campgrounds during the "off-season" periods.

Your food budget is entirely up to you. One of the financial advantages of traveling in an RV is not having to eat every meal in restaurants. Even when we are on the road, I buy a local Sunday paper, cut out the food coupons and take advantage of the sale items.

Look for the free and low-cost attractions available to RVers. We recently visited the Kennedy Space Center in Florida. Parking was free and there was no admission charge. Factory tours can be fun, fascinating and free. Museums, parks and flea markets can provide low cost ways to spend a day. You don't have to spend a lot of money to enjoy yourself.

Joe: These are only a few ideas for controlling your RVing costs. But you get the picture. Once you are past the expense of purchasing a rig, RVing can be a relatively inexpensive pastime.

Fuel Expenses

"We have always used tent trailers for our weekend camping trips and two-week summer vacations. Now that we are about to retire, we are considering buying a motorhome so we can spend more time touring the United States. We are concerned that the cost of fuel will prevent us from traveling to the places we want to go. What kind of fuel mileage can we expect to get?"

Joe: A motorhome's fuel mileage is atrocious when you compare it to driving a compact car. But it's not bad when you consider that you are driving a house.

The important concern is not fuel mileage but whether the motorhome's fuel expenses will prevent you from traveling to the places you want to go.

Let's look at what it would cost you to make your dream come true in a motorhome.

Better yet, let me tell you what Vicki and I have observed from driving a number of both gas and diesel-powered motorhomes across the country. These motorhomes were brand new and from 32 to 37 feet long. They all averaged between eight and ten miles to the gallon of fuel.

By the way, Vicki and I have discovered that, for us, driving becomes tedious after six hours and downright tiresome after eight. We have also concluded that, no matter how fast we drive, at the end of a travel day we seem to have averaged between 45 and 50 miles per hour. A little math tells you that we typically drive no more than 300 to 400 miles a day. Most travel days we actually drive less than 250 miles.

If we drive 400 miles a day and the motorhome gets eight miles to the gallon, we consume about 50 gallons of fuel. If fuel costs $1.20 per gallon, it will cost us about $60 to travel that 400 miles.

The average cost for one night's stay with full hookups in a commercial campground is about $20. Add that to the cost of a day's fuel and it would appear that we are paying $80 a day to travel in a motorhome. Wow!

Vicki: But we don't travel every day. We may only travel for a day or two and then stay put in an interesting spot for two or three days. Some RV travelers remain in one location for a week or longer. When you are not traveling, you do not have any fuel expenses, only your daily campground fees.

To travel the 4,000 miles from Los Angeles to Boston (by way of Seattle or Savannah) we would consume 500 gallons of fuel at a cost of $600.

Even if we drove 400 miles a day, it would take us longer than ten days. Along the way we would spend time exploring San Francisco, the Olympic Peninsula, Yellowstone National Park, Mall of America, Chicago, the Ford automobile assembly plant, the Pro-Football Hall of Fame, the Corning Glass Center and anyplace else that grabbed our fancy.

Getting to Boston would take us at least three weeks. Spread out over that period of time, our motorhome fuel expenses would average out to about $28 per day.

And, because we take advantage of a variety of low-cost overnight spots, our campground costs actually average closer to $15 a day.

Don't let the words "fuel economy" confuse you. Estimate how many miles you'll put on your RV in a year. Then figure out how much money a year's worth of fuel will cost. Now you can decide whether its more important to make your dream come true or to spend that money on something else (and you will spend it).

Membership Campgrounds

"A lot of people have suggested that I join a membership campground. Will you explain how a membership campground works?"

Joe: Covenants and conditions differ among the various membership campground organizations but here is a very simplified explanation:

When you join a membership campground you become entitled to camp free in that campground, which we'll call "home campground", for a limited number of days each year.

You are not purchasing a lot or campsite; only the right, as a member, to use that "home campground".

To join, you pay an initiation (or joining) fee in the thousands of dollars. You also commit yourself to paying dues or a maintenance fee of a few hundred dollars each year. By the way, it is only realistic to expect the annual dues to increase periodically.

The cost of joining may also include finance charges and miscellaneous costs.

If the "home campground" is associated with other membership campgrounds, you may be able to stay in any of that association's campgrounds, usually for a camping fee of a few dollars per day.

This "association" privilege may involve an additional initiation fee and slight increase in your annual dues.

Some membership campground associations have an affiliation with other membership campground associations. For an additional joining fee and additional annual dues you may be able to stay in any of the affiliated association's campgrounds. Again, there will probably be a low daily camping fee.

Vicki: RVers join membership campgrounds for a variety of reasons. The camaraderie of belonging to a group, the feeling of being in a secure environment or the assurance of being able to find a campsite are just a few.

The appeal of membership campgrounds to most RVers, though, is the ability to camp in a large number of campgrounds for a low daily camping fee.

If that's your reason for joining, you'll want to be sure the affiliated membership campgrounds will be available to you.

There may be a requirement that in order for you to use an affiliated campground or receive the low daily rate, it has to be located a certain distance, perhaps a hundred miles or more, from your "home campground".

Some RVers buy into a "home campground" located in a distant, remote location so they are able to use the various affiliated campgrounds closer to home.

Also, check to be sure there are affiliated membership campgrounds along the roads you will travel and in the areas you are likely to visit.

There's no point in belonging to a membership campground if you're not going to be staying in their campgrounds.

Joe: Do some math if your objective in joining a membership campground is to reduce your camping expenses. Figure out how many nights you will have to stay in membership campgrounds, as opposed to non-membership campgrounds, to really save money.

Prices vary but let's say, for example, the initiation (joining fee) in a national affiliation of membership campgrounds costs about $6,000 and the current annual dues are $300 per year. Let's also assume you will use the membership for ten years.

The initiation fee ($6,000 divided by 10 years) would amount to $600 per year. The annual dues would add another $300 per year. Using these figures, it would cost $900 per year to maintain a campground membership.

A non-membership campground charges about $25 per night for an equivalent campsite.

Dividing this $25 into the $900 annual cost of campground membership means you could stay in non-membership campgrounds for 36 nights each year for what it would cost to belong to a membership campground.

This computation does not take into consideration the interest you would have to pay to finance the $6,000 initiation fee or the interest the $6,000 would earn if it remained in your bank account. Nor does it reflect the possibility of assessments and periodic increases in annual dues. It also ignores the probability of increased overnight camping fees at both membership and non-membership campgrounds.

But it does give you a formula to determine if belonging to a membership campground would make financial sense to you.

In this case, if you think that during the next ten years you will spend more than 36 nights per year in membership campgrounds, it might make good financial sense to join one.

There's also a possibility (but no guarantee) that you could sell your membership at the end of the ten-year period. That would further reduce the overall cost of membership.

Look at the classified section of RV magazines under "Membership Campground Resales" to get an idea of what people are *asking* for their memberships. Resale competition can be pretty keen.

Vicki: Check out a number of competing membership campgrounds before buying. Visit or, better yet, spend a couple nights in what would be your "home campground". Talk to the members. Ask them if they would recommend joining. Do they have any difficulty making reservations? What is the financial condition of the campground?

Listen to the sales presentations. Ask questions. Take notes.

Membership campgrounds sustain themselves by selling memberships. What is the ratio of members to campsites at the "home campground" you are considering joining? Are non-members, in addition to members of affiliated associations, allowed to camp in your "home campground"? How difficult will it be for you to make reservations in your "home campground"?

Find out if you would be allowed to sell your membership during the first few years of ownership. Are there transfer fees or other costs involved in selling your membership? How many times may the membership be resold? Can it be passed on in your estate?

How do you cancel your membership? What are the financial ramifications if you stop paying the annual dues?

What happens to your membership in the affiliated campgrounds and associations if your "home campground" goes bankrupt? Will you lose your investment?

Take home, scrutinize and compare the literature and copies of the contracts.

Joining a membership campground should complement your RVing needs, make financial sense and enhance your enjoyment of RVing.

Investigate before you invest.

Safety And Security

"Do you feel safe out there? Do you carry a gun?"

Joe: What these folks are really asking is, *"Aren't you afraid of becoming a crime victim?"* and *"What can we do to protect our valuables and ourselves?"*

Our standard reply is that we feel just as safe in our RV as we do at home. Maybe safer.

It would be foolish to think that we are completely safe while RVing. Nothing is completely 100 percent safe.

Actually, life is full of risks. House fires occur every day; yet you sleep in a house most nights. Automobiles are constantly involved in accidents; but you continue to drive every day. An earthquake or meteorite could suddenly destroy the building you're in; but there you sit.

These are a sample of the risks we acknowledge, accept and deal with every day of our lives. Life is full of risks.

Traveling in an RV also has risks; we wouldn't attempt to tell you otherwise. But we will tell you that when you are RVing, you are living in a relatively low-crime neighborhood.

Before we look at that neighborhood, let's look at the criminal. As with everything, there are exceptions and extremes but, generally, the criminal is an opportunist looking for an easy target, a fast grab and a quick getaway.

Think about it. The burglar prefers to take your valuables when you aren't there to protect them; the petty thief steals when you're not aware of his presence and the con artist strikes when he can take advantage of your ignorance. The purse snatcher, mugger and armed robber rely upon force or fear to control their victims.

Whatever their mode of operation, all of these criminals select an easy or vulnerable target. They move quickly and make their escape as soon as possible.

Obviously, the criminal would prefer to pass over a target that is difficult to control or could result in him getting hurt or caught.

Vicki: Now let's look at the RV neighborhood. Generally speaking, the RVer is not an easy target subject to a fast grab.

RV destinations and campgrounds are seldom located in what would be considered high-crime areas. Oh, we have stayed in a few big city RV parks with security patrols and fences topped with barbed wire but they are few and far between. One of the appeals of most RV destinations is the fact that they are located in relatively low-crime areas.

RVers generally park in close proximity to other RVers. And there always seems to be at least one couple sitting outside who seems interested in everything that's going on around them. Non-campers are pretty easy to spot and, as a result, they attract attention to themselves.

And you never know when a ranger, camp host or strolling camper will pass by. These are people who could come to an RVer's aid or act as witnesses. Criminals prefer to avoid the inconvenience involved with getting caught.

It's difficult to establish patterns of movement or occupancy in and around RVs. We come and go unpredictably. You can't be sure if the RV occupants are gone and you never know when they will return. That person walking up the road might be the owner of that RV, his friend or the campground owner.

It's also not easy to determine who, what or how many may be inside an RV. It could be a lineman for the Rams, a snarling Great Dane or a little, old lady with a big, new gun. Criminals have the same aversion to pain as everyone else.

And, an RV, because its windows are higher off the ground, can be more difficult to break into than a house.

As you can see, RVers, by virtue of their lifestyle, do not present an easy target for a quick grab and a fast getaway.

Joe: There are some common sense things you can do to further minimize the risks of becoming a crime victim

Harden the target. Install good locks and get in the habit of using them. If you don't already have one, put a deadbolt lock on your RV's entry door. Upgrade the locks on the exterior storage bays.

By the way, it's not a bad idea to rekey your factory-installed deadbolt lock. There are a lot of master keys floating around. And, of course, you should have a locksmith rekey the deadbolt and other locks whenever you purchase a previously owned RV.

A hitch lock will discourage anyone from hooking up to your trailer and driving away.

Back up the latches in sliding windows by placing metal or wooden rods in the channel at the base of the window.

Use a light chain or cable to secure bicycles, barbecues and other outdoor items to the picnic table or RV bumper.

Store your cash and valuables in a hidden safe or lockbox inside your RV.

Install exterior lights that can be turned on from the interior of your rig. Use manual, not sensing, lights. Sensing lights go on and off all night. Your neighbors either ignore them or soon begin to hope that you do get robbed.

If you install an alarm, advertise the fact, and spend the extra bucks for one you can personally activate if you need help.

A dog that barks when strangers approach (but only when strangers approach) is a great deterrent.

Vicki: Avoid becoming a target. An RVer can be vulnerable when his rig suffers a roadside breakdown, especially at night. The risk of a breakdown can be minimized with a good program of preventative maintenance. The only way to completely avoid breaking down at night, though, is to travel during daylight.

Carry a cellular phone so you can call for help in an emergency. Stop by the welcome center of each state you visit. Ask what number you should dial on your cellular phone in case of an emergency. While you are there, pick up a state map. Most state maps will list the telephone numbers you can call in an emergency.

Know where you are. Develop the habit of knowing your location. Help will arrive a lot sooner if you can tell the police dispatcher your highway number, direction of travel (northbound, southbound, etc.) and the nearest milepost marker or exit number.

Keep in mind that using your CB radio to call for help also notifies everyone else of your situation and location.

It's a difficult judgment call as to whether you should get out of your disabled rig when a stranger stops and offers to help. One option is to stay in the safety of your vehicle and ask the stranger to call the Highway Patrol or your emergency roadside service.

Be wary of strangers telling you to stop because your RV has a problem. Drive to the nearest occupied rest area to check for RV troubles.

Traveling with other RVers gives you safety in numbers and the security of someone to help you during any type of problem.

Avoid any place where you do not feel comfortable or your intuition tells you is unsafe, especially when you're considering spending the night.

Camp within eyesight of other RVers. Make a point of saying "hello" to neighboring campers. They will be more inclined to pay attention to strangers around your rig.

Don't show off computers, cellular phones, wads of cash or other tempting, easy to steal items.

Draw the blinds at night. There's no point in revealing who and or what is inside your RV.

Don't put a sign on your rig advertising your name. That makes it easy for someone to knock on your door and call out your name(s) as though you were acquainted.

Don't open the door without visually checking out callers. Talk to them through an open window.

Be wary of strangers who want to see the inside of your rig because they're "thinking about buying one".

Put a light on a timer and play a radio when you are gone. Just like you do when you are home. And don't leave notes saying you're not in the campground and when you'll return.

Generally speaking, when you are RVing, you are in a low-crime neighborhood. Use common sense, listen to your instincts and you can further reduce the risks of becoming an easy target for a fast grab and a quick getaway.

Joe: People we don't know frequently ask if we carry a gun in our RV. I'm concerned that if I answer "yes", they may be tempted to steal it, and if I answer "no" they will think we are a vulnerable target. So, I politely respond, "If you really want to know, kick in my door and step inside".

Everyone then assumes I am a bloodthirsty, gun-loving, redneck just itching for an opportunity to blow someone's head off. An image I don't agree with but see no point in discouraging.

There's a lot of discussion these days about carrying a gun in an RV. I'd like to contribute my observations. The purpose of a gun is to kill. If you're not prepared to take someone's life, perhaps you should think twice about carrying a gun.

Police officers receive hours and hours of professional training on the use of deadly force. And they occasionally make fatal mistakes. If you do decide to carry a gun, please take a thorough training course on how and when to use it. More importantly, learn when not to use it. After all, I might be parked next door to you some night.

By the way, if you decide to carry a handgun in your RV, familiarize yourself with the handgun laws of the cities, counties, states and nations you plan on visiting.

Vicki: Generally speaking, the RV world is a low-crime neighborhood. Obviously, Joe and I feel quite comfortable out there. Our comfort level comes from knowing that RVers are generally not perceived as targets of opportunity.

We also use common sense to avoid becoming crime victims. And then, there's this odd perception people have about my husband that he sees no point in discouraging.

Traveling With Pets

"We want to travel in our RV with our two dogs. Any advice?"

Joe: A lot of RVers take their dogs, cats and other household pets on the road. Vicki and I frequently see RVs with two or three dogs and/or cats.

We have even shared campgrounds with dog-sled enthusiasts. These folks travel with a half-dozen or more dogs. The animals are very well behaved and their owners set an example in campground etiquette we wish other pet owners would follow.

Most, but not all, RV parks and government campgrounds accept dogs and cats. Don't be surprised, however, if there is an extra charge for your pet. You may even be assigned to an area of the campground designated for pet owners.

The campground will ask you to clean up after your pet, keep it on a leash and not allow it to disturb your neighbors. RV pet owners who think these rules do not apply to them are the reason some RV parks and campgrounds now refuse to allow pets.

Vicki: Some dogs and cats, like human beings, readily adapt and even look forward to RV travel while others have difficulty adjusting.

Keep in mind, your animals will be barraged by new sights, sounds and smells. They will be in close contact with a variety of strange people and surroundings. This can be stressful for some dogs and may lead to barking and unpredictable behavior.

It may be a good idea to accustom your pets to RVing by taking them on short trips at first, then gradually increasing the length of time they spend on the road and in campgrounds.

Try to locate a permanent place in the RV for the animal's food and water bowls.

Provide a protective travel case for your pets. It will keep them from jumping on or otherwise interfering with the driver. It will also prevent them from becoming flying missiles when the brakes are suddenly applied. The travel case can double as a familiar and secure place for your pet to sleep.

Joe: You'll want to carry a valid rabies vaccination certificate. Many government campgrounds and some RV parks require them. RVers traveling to and from Canada and Mexico are required to have a valid veterinarian health certificate, including a proof of rabies vaccination.

Be prepared in case your dog or cat gets away from you. Put an identification collar on it. Include your RV's make and license number as well as your RV's cellular phone number. You might ask your veterinarian about identification tattoos and under-the-skin implants. Check into the lost pet service offered by RV clubs.

Carry a leash for exercising and some type of tethering rope or chain to keep your pet within the confines of your campsite.

By the way, don't leave your animal tethered and unattended outside the RV. Unable to flee, it would be easy prey for a wild animal. And you certainly wouldn't want your dog to attack a child who suddenly ran through your campsite.

Vicki: Think about what you will do with your pet when you are not able to take it with you for the day. You don't want to leave it unattended in a hot or unventilated RV. A vent fan or air conditioner can be left running, but what if there is a power failure?

Some campgrounds and recreation destinations offer "day-care" kennels. Before you drop your pet off for the day, inspect the premises. Ask what protective measures they take against parasites, infection and distemper.

Take care of your animal's health. Mosquitoes transmit heartworm. Ticks and fleas abound in outdoor areas. Ask your veterinarian about preventatives.

Be aware that strange food and water could cause digestive upset. This is not the time to alter your pet's diet.

Pet odors can build rapidly in the confined space of an RV. You'll want to work diligently to minimize odors and prevent fleas.

Finally, be a good neighbor. Clean up your pet's waste. Keep it on a leash. And please, don't permit it to bark, whine or otherwise disturb the RVers around you.

RV Travel Tips

"We have only used our travel trailer for weekends and vacations at nearby campgrounds. This summer we want to spend our three-week vacation traveling around neighboring states. This will be our first RV travel trip. Any helpful tips?"

Vicki: The best time of year to travel is during the "shoulder" months of May, June, September and October. These months experience mild weather and less travelers throughout most of the country.

The best weekends to travel are just before a holiday weekend. Everyone is getting ready for the holiday.

The best days to arrive at a campground are late Sunday and anytime Monday. All the weekenders will have just left and there will be plenty of sites available.

Plan your trip using detailed road maps with time and mileage indicators. Automobile clubs are excellent sources of good maps. We've found that traveling in an RV generally takes about ten percent longer than the time indicated on maps.

Use a highlighter pen to mark your route on the map. When choosing your travel route, try to avoid the heavy traffic of big cities and the engine strain of steep mountain passes.

Every major population center has its "rush hour". Select your route and time your travels to avoid getting caught in commuter traffic. Don't overlook the possibility of heavy weekend traffic if you travel late Friday or Sunday afternoons.

Joe: Most RVs are designed to maintain a comfortable highway cruising speed of 55 miles per hour. Many RVers drive faster but, by the end of the day, most generally average 45 to 50 miles per hour. So, no matter how fast you drive, when planning your travel day, figure that you'll average 45 to 50 miles per hour on the main highways.

Seasoned RV travelers have discovered that driving between four and six hours each day is a much more comfortable pace. It allows them to stop at interesting spots, enjoy a leisurely lunch and arrive at their destination in a relaxed frame of mind.

While an occasional long driving day is OK, try to keep your actual driving time to less than six hours per day. It may take some attitude adjusting, but you and your family will enjoy your travels a lot more.

Drive during the early hours of the day. Your mind is fresh and clear. Driving into the morning sun is less brutal than driving into the afternoon sun. You'll avoid the heat of the day and winds will be less of a problem. Driving through hot deserts and up mountain grades during the cool early hours of the day is also easier on your rig's engine.

Take a break every couple of hours. Walk you rig. Look underneath for leaks, check the condition of your tires, be sure the trailer hitch and connections are secure.

Vicki: Make your lunch break a fun part of the travel day. Roadside rest areas are convenient, but a city park or playground will be a treat for the kids. Historical sites have plenty of parking space and give you an opportunity to stretch your legs. We like to combine lunch with a visit to a local tourist attraction or a factory that offers tours.

Lunch is also a good time to open your campground and RV park directory, look ahead and line up a couple of overnight camping destinations. If your first choice doesn't work out, you'll have an alternative.

Stop at each state's welcome center. Look for them in rest areas as you cross from one state to the next. Welcome centers usually have racks of informative brochures that have been placed there by commercial interests, tourist attractions and campgrounds.

Joe: Check out a travel plaza when it's time to refuel. Once known as truck stops, travel plazas are courting the business of RV travelers. Travel plazas offer gasoline and diesel fuel, convenience stores, restaurants and restrooms. Many have even installed dump stations and easy-access RV fuel islands.

Plan on getting off the road by four or five in the afternoon. RV parks and campgrounds will have more vacancies. There'll be time to go for a walk, take a swim or treat yourself to a nap.

Vicki: Take advantage of the campground laundry rooms. Here is where you get, firsthand, all the latest and the best information.

RVers have a tendency to chat while waiting for their clothes to wash and dry. There's an excellent chance the person sharing the laundry room with you has just come from the direction in which you're heading.

They can tell you their impressions of campgrounds, attractions and road conditions they have encountered.

Some of the best travel tips and money-saving advice we've received has come from RVers we've met in campground laundry rooms.

Making Money On The Road

"Is it possible to generate some kind of income while traveling?"

Joe: We're seeing more and more RVers who are combining their love of RV travel with making money on the road. While many are fulltimers, some are extended RV travelers who live in a house between their income generating trips.

These RVers find ways of making money either as independent business people or by working for others. There's no reason why you can't be one of them.

First, look at your objectives. Think about why you want to make money on the road. Do you need to make a living or just supplement your existing income? Do you want to offset your travel expenses or are you simply interested in making a casual dollar?

Next, sit down with your travel partner and decide how much time and effort you wish to devote to making money. Try to strike a balance between the time you spend working and the time available to enjoy your travels.

Finally, ask yourself what you want to do to make money on the road. Do you want to be in business for yourself or work for others?

Vicki: Being in business for yourself means you have the freedom to choose your working location, atmosphere and hours. You are in control. You are the boss.

Being in business for yourself also means investing the time and money to establish your business. You'll have to deal with business permits, sales taxes and insurance. You may also have to deal with late payments, bounced checks and collections. And then there's the paperwork ...

Do some research. Your local library is loaded with books about starting a home-based business. And that, essentially, is what your "on the road" business will be.

Starting and operating an on-the-road business is the same as any other business but RVers have a few additional considerations.

You'll be conducting business in different locations. Ascertain whether you or your business will require a professional license, sales permit or special certification from local government agencies in each new location. Repeating this procedure and expense every time you move could be prohibitive.

It's a rare business that is not dependent upon a telephone. Telephone hookups are not commonplace in RV parks so plan on using pay phones frequently. Get a telephone calling card and don't overlook the money saving potential of pre-paid phone cards.

A telephone answering machine at home or some sort of voice-mail service will be a necessity. You'll find a pager is a good tool and a cellular phone can be a definite asset. Remember, long distance calls can add up and cellular calls are very expensive, especially while roaming.

Joe: Research who your customers will be and how you will contact them while you are on the road.

One way to reach customers is to rent a vendor's booth at the thousands of trade shows, fairs, rallies and flea markets that take place around the country.

We have seen RVers selling RV accessories, crafts, wooden signs, custom name badges, herbs, antiques and even flagpoles in these vendor booths.

We are acquainted with one fulltiming couple who supplement their retirement income by selling windchimes at RV shows, rallies and fairs. They carry their inventory and display materials in their motorhome's storage bays. Sometimes they set up under the awning of their RV; other times they set up inside a vendor's building or tent. Years of trial and error have helped them develop a circuit that takes them to the fairs and shows that provide the best income.

If you're going to sell a product, decide how and where you will receive, transport and store that product while you're on the road. Keep in mind that heavy or bulky items may exceed your RV's carrying capability.

Providing a service is one way to avoid inventory and sales taxes. If you presently have a service business, see if there's a way you can take it on the road.

We met a woman who specialized in doing portraits of couples standing in front of their RVs. She took Polaroid photos of them in campgrounds and worked from that. Most of her customers were so pleased with her work, they asked her to do portraits of their grandchildren or pets.

Are you an entertainer? Musicians, magicians, mimes, clowns and ventriloquists find work at trade shows, fairs and special events all around the country.

Vicki: You may be among the many RVers who prefer to avoid business headaches by working for someone else. You will receive a regular paycheck and may even qualify for employee benefits. Best of all, you will only be committed to a pre-determined type of work for an established period of time.

There seem to be more job opportunities available for RVers than there are RVers willing to fill them. Most of these jobs are temporary or seasonal in nature. That means you will have plenty of opportunity to enjoy your travels between jobs.

Commercial campgrounds and RV parks frequently hire RVers, especially during their busy seasons. Jobs include office work, security, recreation and maintenance. Many of the opportunities are for couples. Compensation, in addition to a salary, usually includes a free campsite and discounts at the campground store.

National parks concessionaires hire thousands of RVers every year to operate their hotels, gas stations, grocery stores, gift shops and restaurants.

You'll find openings for tour guides, drivers, maintenance workers, accountants, personnel clerks, computer operators, managers, medical, hotel and restaurant people.

Seasonal jobs are not limited to the great outdoors. The gambling casinos around the country hire RVers as dealers, change makers, security guards, cooks, waitresses, musicians and entertainers.

Pumpkin patches and Christmas tree lots hire RVers. They typically pay a weekly salary and provide a water and electric hookup for your RV right there on the lot. No long commute here.

During the Christmas season, RVers find work as department store Santa Clauses, sales clerks and gift wrappers. And, somebody must paint all those attractive decorations on the store windows.

When you're tired of spreading joy and cheer at the end of one year, you can find work as a tax preparer during the first few months of the next year.

Being an RVer is actually an advantage when looking for seasonal work.

Lots of RVers make a living, supplement their existing income or offset their travel expenses. Either by being in business for themselves or working for others. They are making money on the road. They are making their dreams come true. You can too!

Working On The Road

"We will soon retire and hope to RV fulltime for a few years. Initially we will travel to all those places we have been reading about. Then we plan to locate a new retirement home by staying in selected communities and working for a few months at a time. Can you tell me about getting temporary work while fulltiming?"

Joe: It sounds like you are taking a logical approach to enjoying your retirement. We've talked to a number of people who, like you, want to travel extensively for a while but then re-establish their roots.

Getting a temporary job will not only augment your retirement income, it will give you an opportunity to become a part of the community to see if it fits your retirement needs.

Finding temporary work while fulltiming is not difficult. In fact it appears there are more jobs looking for RVers than there are RVers looking for jobs.

Commercial campgrounds and RV parks frequently employ RVers during their busy seasons. Jobs include office work, security, recreation and maintenance.

Compensation often includes a free campsite with hookups and a salary commensurate with the type and amount of work you will be doing. Since most of these jobs are temporary or seasonal in nature, you will have plenty of opportunity to explore the country between jobs.

One nice thing about working in campgrounds, you are there during the most pleasant time of the year.

Once you have gained some experience working in a campground or RV park you'll find your services in demand almost everywhere you go.

Vicki: Check out the temporary help agencies. Temporary help agencies are no longer limited to clerical or office positions. These companies now find temporary positions for men and women of all ages in every conceivable field.

Accountants, assembly-line workers, bank employees, draftsmen, engineers, executives, nurses, paralegals and pharmacists are just a few of those who can find work through a temporary help agency.

Here's a tip: Establish a good track record with a temporary help agency that has offices nationwide. When you are ready to move to the next community, ask the agency to FAX your records to their office closest to your destination. You'll have your paperwork done and a good recommendation waiting when you arrive. They might even have a job lined up for you.

Joe: Don't overlook the general employment market. Scour the want ads, contact the local chamber of commerce, check out the bulletin boards at colleges and local libraries.

Search the trade and professional magazines for ads and ideas. See if anyone is looking for vacation relief or work overload personnel.

Vicki: America is a beautiful country. Its going to be difficult deciding where you want to settle down. So enjoy the search for your new retirement home. But be careful. You may find a new career while you're at it.

RV Show Vendors

"My husband and I recently attended an RV show being held at a county fairground. We noticed a number of RVs that appeared to be camped in one section of the parking lot. Who were these people?"

Joe: The RVs may have belonged to some of the show's exhibitors and vendors. A good number of the folks who set up a display or sales booth at an RV show are RVers. They are among the thousands of RVers who have found a way to make money on the road.

Typically, the vendors arrive the day before the show opens. Display materials and/or sales merchandise will be unloaded from a travel trailer's tow vehicle, the storage bays of a motorhome or, in some cases, an equipment trailer being pulled by a motorhome. The balance of the day is spent setting up their booth or display. The vendors live in their RVs right there at the RV show.

The vendors hope to make enough money during the show to cover their travel and living expenses, pay for the rent on their booth space, recoup their investment in merchandise and, with a little luck, make a profit.

They know their fortunes depend upon the professional skills of the show promoter, the mood of the crowd, the whims of the weather and their own ability to attract and convince customers to buy.

Vicki: While a few vendors are casual sellers of merchandise, most are serious business people. They know which shows and promoters are likely to bring them the greatest return on their investment. Many work a circuit of shows and rallies that keep their down time to a minimum.

Don't be surprised to see a vendor pass your credit card through a card reader connected to a cellular phone. This is the twentieth century and they are very much a part of it.

At the end of the last day of the show the vendors break down their displays and store them in their vehicles. Some may even head down the road that evening. They have another show ahead of them.

Talk to a show vendor during a quiet moment. He may give you some insight into his lifestyle. You might even find yourself the owner of a gadget you never knew you needed.

Missing The Grandchildren

"**We've recently retired, and my husband wants to spend three months traveling around the country in our RV. I can't imagine being away from my grandchildren for such a long time. What tips do you have for making the separation easier? Won't the little ones forget who we are?**"

Vicki: This is a question we're frequently asked. We moms and grandmas do seem to have a hard time being away from our chicks. Many dads and grandpas feel the same way, they just don't admit it as readily as we do. It must be a "guy" thing--kind of like not wanting to ask directions at a gas station.

Joe and I are part of the "sandwich" generation. We are concerned about not only our children and grandchildren, but our parents as well. Our grandchildren are very young and we especially miss them when we're on the road.

We stay in touch on a regular basis while traveling. Using pay phones and a calling card we call our parents and each of our children every weekend.

We always try to call our kids at a time when we think our grandkids will be able to come to the phone. Sometimes it becomes a real challenge when we're in different time zones.

These calls give us a chance to hear the recent news and make sure everyone is all right. This is also our opportunity to let everyone know that we're okay, too. We've discovered that our family gets concerned about us. Especially when they are aware of severe weather near our location.

Cellular phone calls cost a lot when traveling so we restrict ours to emergency use only. Our kids know that if they want to let us know about an emergency at home, they can call us on the cellphone. If they want to talk to us about a non-emergency, they leave a message on our answering machine. Otherwise, they just wait to talk to us when we call on weekends.

Here are some ways to get your "grandchildren fix" and keep the little ones from forgetting who you are.

Make sure to place those phone calls at a time when you can talk to the grandchildren, and start when they are babies.

When our grandaughter, Amanda, was just eight months old, we left on a three-month trip. Each week when we called, Joe and I both talked to our daughter. Then I always asked her to put Amanda on the phone.

Standing there at a public telephone, sounding like a complete fool to anyone passing by, I carried on a one-sided conversation with that baby. No matter how hard I tried, however, I couldn't convince Joe to make a fool of himself too. It must have been that "guy" thing.

When we got home and Amanda heard my voice, she came right into my arms. Joe's voice, though, wasn't familiar and she held back a little until she got used to him. Guess who now makes a fool of himself at pay phones!

Make a video tape. This is a great tool for communicating with your grandchildren while you are gone. All you need is a camcorder and a VCR.

We had to miss Amanda's third birthday a few years ago. Before we left home, we taped ourselves talking to her and singing, "Happy Birthday". We gave her mom the tape and asked her to play it at the birthday party. From what we hear, that tape was played so many times that everyone except Amanda got very tired of it.

We took another long trip when our grandson, Kevin, was a year old. Before we left, our daughter-in-law asked if she could make a videotape of us sitting on the couch and talking to Kevin just as though we were there with him.

She played that tape almost every day while we were gone. When we got home, he acted as though we had never been away.

You can make video tapes of yourselves talking to your family wherever you go. Pick an interesting background, prop the camera up, step into the picture and start talking.

Camera and stationary stores have padded envelopes made for shipping video tapes.

Send postcards. All kids love to get mail. It makes them feel important. Starting when they were about three years old, we have sent Amanda and Kevin postcards once a week while we are traveling. It doesn't matter if they can't read; "Papa" signs his cards with a cartoon caricature of himself. The kids always know who is sending them mail.

We always seem to end up discussing the pictures on the front of the postcards when we make our weekly calls. Our grandchildren consider us "mail" symbols! We have not yet sent e-mail to them, but I'm sure that day will come.

We can see ourselves spending more and more time making videos, talking on pay phones and writing postcards in the future. Our newest addition, Daniel, was born in February and we expect another granddaughter, Nicole, in July. No matter how much time or effort it takes, hearing those little voices at the other end of the phone and the greeting we get at homecoming makes it all worth it.

Go. You and your husband enjoy each other and your RV journey. Just be sure to keep in touch while you are on the road. Your little ones won't forget you.

Familiar Places

"Don't you miss the comfort of familiar surroundings when you're away from home?"

Joe: Until you asked the question, we thought the reason we traveled was to escape our familiar surroundings. We thoroughly enjoy discovering and exploring new places and getting acquainted with new people. But, now that we think about it, we do find ourselves gravitating to the comfort of familiar surroundings all over the country.

The nationwide chains and franchises have allowed the entire United States to become our neighborhood.

Vicki: We know, for example, that the quality and type of facilities at KOAs all over the country is pretty consistent. We can count on finding fuel islands reserved for RVers at Flying J Travel Plazas and we know that Camping World stores can repair or service our rig.

We find Wal-Mart and K-Mart stores just about everywhere we go. It's an unusual mall that doesn't have a Sears, Radio Shack and a Hallmark shop. Kroger and Safeway markets offer familiar comfort when grocery shopping and we have also gotten to know the regional favorites like the Fred Meyer stores in the northwest.

Joe: We go to Kinko's and Staples for office supplies and business services; Home Depot and Ace for hardware items; Napa and Kragen for auto parts.

My favorite neighborhood places have names like McDonald's, Cracker Barrel and Lone Star Steak House. And when I'm in the mood for international cuisine we look for Pizza Hut, Taco Bell and International House Of Pancakes.

Vicki: So, you see, we are never very far from the comfort of familiar surroundings but we still enjoy discovering and exploring that corner grocery store or the mom and pop shops. They just seem to add to the adventure of being an RVer.

Information To Go

"Where can I go in my RV? What is there to see and do? How do I get there?"

One of the keys to successful RVing is knowing how and where to get the answers to these questions.

A variety of information sources are available for avid RVers. Here are a few to get you started.

Campground and/or RV Park Directory - A campground directory is a basic RVing necessity. It provides an easy-to-follow system of maps and alphabetical listings which enable you to identify the overnight facilities located in the area you wish to stay.

Each campground listing provides the name, phone number and directions to the campground from the nearest main highway. A description of the campground, its facilities and fees helps you select the one suited to your needs and budget. Finally, a rating system gives you an idea of the quality, completeness and cleanliness of the facilities.

Some campground directories, like *Trailer Life's Campgrounds, RV Parks & Services Directory*, provide additional information such as state highway laws regulating RVs, bridge, tunnel and ferry restrictions as well as the locations of disposal stations along major highways.

Most RVers travel with two or three different campground directories.

RV Magazines - Subscribe to at least one RV magazine. You'll be able to read about interesting places to go and things to see and do. "How-to" articles provide good information on improving, maintaining and repairing your rig. Technical and lifestyle experts respond to reader inquiries. Letters to the editor provide insight into the thoughts, complaints and quandaries of subscribers.

You'll also find the latest in RV books and other sources of information publicized or advertised in these magazines.

We recommend you subscribe to both a nationwide and a regional magazine. The nationwide will give you a broad perspective on the issues. The regional will provide you with information about camping destinations and RV services close to home.

Newspaper and Magazine Travel Sections - Although they may not be RV specific, many articles will be of interest to the RV traveler. Start saving those articles about places that interest you. We maintain a file folder for each state and refer to it when we are planning our travels.

RV Clubs - Join at least one nationwide RV club.
Among the largest are:
    Good Sam RV Owners Club (800-234-3450)
    Escapees RV Club (888-SKP-CLUB)
    Family Motor Coach Association (800-543-3622)
These RV clubs offer insurance programs, emergency roadside services and discounts at campgrounds. Membership also includes a periodic magazine with informative articles and columns.

Local RV clubs schedule weekend trips throughout the year. What better way to discover the campgrounds available in your area.

Brand name RV clubs are excellent sources of RV information and ideas. If you have a question about your RV, chances are that someone in that club who owns a similar model will know the answer.

Attend RV club rallies. They feature educational seminars by experts in every RV subject imaginable.

Automobile Clubs - The American Automobile Association, for example, is an excellent source for road maps and tour books. Members may also avail themselves of a trip routing service called Triptic. A Triptic is a series of loosely bound strip maps. They provide detailed information about the road, terrain and points of interest along your chosen route.

RV Accessory Store or Catalog - Most RV accessory stores will have a magazine and book rack. RV books not normally found in bookstores will be on display here. RV accessory catalogs offer RVing books and will keep you abreast of the latest in accessories and gadgets.

Libraries and Bookstores - It seems obvious, but many people overlook these treasure troves of information. Look under Camping, Motorhomes, Recreation, Recreation Vehicles and Travel Trailers. While you are there, look in the library's travel section for information on every state and tourist destination.

Computer Internet Web Sites - There are a variety of web sites offering information from RV manufacturers, dealers, campgrounds, clubs and more. An excellent starting point is our own **www.rvknowhow.com**

Computer On-line Services - Find out which online services offer RV forums. RV enthusiasts exchange experience, advice and ideas. RV manufacturers, dealers, service centers and publications participate in "discussions" and help with questions and problems.

Computer Software Stores - Mapping and travel software is available for computer owners. RVers can plot their trips based upon the quickest, shortest or most scenic route.

Government Travel and Camping Information - Contact the National Park Service, National Forest Service, U.S. Fish and Wildlife Service, Bureau of Land Management and U.S. Army Corps of Engineers for information about camping on public lands.

Check your campground directory for the address of each state's bureau of tourism. Send to them for state maps, campground directories and travel information.

County Parks and Recreation Departments, located in the county seat, can provide information about their county's camping opportunities.

Visitor Welcome Centers - Most states provide a visitor welcome center near their borders. Look for them in rest areas as you cross from one state to the next. Welcome centers will house racks of informative brochures placed there by commercial interests.

After perusing the brochure racks, go to the counter and ask for a state road map, state parks & campground directory and any other specialized information you can't find in the open. Often the best stuff is located behind the counter.

Travel Plazas (truck stops) - Travel plazas are courting the business of RV travelers. Some, like Flying J Travel Plazas, have even installed RV fuel islands for easy access. Visit their convenience stores and check out their magazine and book racks. You'll discover that the map and travel information needs of truckers is very similar to those of RVers.

Campground Stores - Their magazine, book and brochure racks may have information about RVs, RVing and local places of interest.

Campground Laundry Rooms - Here is where you get, firsthand, all the latest and the best information. RVers have a tendency to chat while waiting for their clothes to wash and dry. There's an excellent chance the person sharing the laundry room with you has just come from the direction you're heading. They can tell you their impressions of road conditions, campgrounds and attractions they have encountered. Some of our best tips and money-saving advice has come from people we've met in campground laundry rooms.

Government Travel and Camping Information

Send for camping information on public lands.

Bureau of Land Management
Public Affairs Office
1849 C Street NW
Washington, DC 20240

National Forest Service
U.S. Department of Agriculture
Office of Information
P.O. Box 96090
Washington, DC 20090

National Park Service
1849 C Street, NW
MS-1013
Washington, DC 20240

National Wildlife Refuges
U.S. Fish and Wildlife Service
Public Affairs Office
1849 C Street, NW
Publications Department WEB
Room 130
Washington, DC 20240

U.S. Army Corps of Engineers
OCE Publications Depot
2803 52nd Avenue
Hyattsville, MD 20781-1102

State Tourism Bureaus

Alabama Bureau of Tourism
1-800-ALABAMA
www.state.al.us

Alaska Division of Tourism
1-800-76 ALASKA
www.state.ak.us/tourism

Alaska Marine Hwy System
1-800-642-0066
www.dot.state.ak.us

Arizona Office of Tourism
1-800-842-8257
www.arizonaguide.com

Arkansas Tourism Office
1-800-NATURAL
www.state.arkansas.com

California Office of Tourism
1-800-TO CALIF
www.gocalif.ca.gov

Colorado Tourism Board
1-800-COLORADO
www.colorado.com

Connecticut Div of Tourism
1-800-CT BOUND
www.state.ct.us/tourism

Delaware Tourism Office
1-800-441- 8846
www.state.de.us/tourism

Florida Div. of Tourism
1-888-7 FLA USA
www.flausa.com

Georgia Dept of Tourism
1-800-VISIT GA
www.gomm.com

Idaho Div of Tourism
1-800-VISIT ID
www.visitid.org

Illinois Bureau of Tourism
1-800-2 CONNECT
www.enjoyillinois.com

Indiana Dept.of Tourism
1-800-289-6646
www.state.in.us/tourism

Iowa Div. of Tourism
1-800-345-IOWA
www.state.ia.us/tourism

Kansas Travel Division
1-800-252-6727
www.kansascommerce.com

Kentucky Dept. of Travel
1-800-225-TRIP
www.state.ky.us/tour

Louisiana Tourism
1-800-33-GUMBO
www.crt.state.la.us/tourism

Maine Office of Tourism
1-800-533-9595
www.visitmaine.com

Maryland Tourism
1-800-MD IS FUN
www.mdisfun.org

Massachusetts Tourism
1-800-447-MASS
www.massvacation.com

Michigan Travel Bureau
1-800-644-7669
www.michigan.org

Minnesota Tourism
1-800-657-3700
www.exploreminnesota.com

Mississippi Tourism
1-800-WARMEST
www. state.ms.us/

Missouri Tourism
1-800-877-1234
www.missouritourism.org

Montana Travel
1-800-VISIT MT
www.travel.mt.gov

Nebraska Tourism
1-800-228-4307
www.visitnebraska.org

Nevada Tourism
1-800-NEVADA8
www.travel.nevada.com

New Hampshire Travel
1-800-FUN IN NH
www.visitnh.gov

New Jersey Tourism
1-800-JERSEY 7
www.state.nj.us/travel

New Mexico Tourism
1-800-545-2040
www.newmexico.org

New York Tourism
1-800-CALL NYS
www.iloveny.state.ny.us

North Carolina Tourism
1-800-VISIT-NC
www.visitnc.com

North Dakota Tourism
1-800-HELLO-ND
www.ndtourism.com

Ohio Tourism
1-800-BUCKEYE
www.ohiotourism.com

Oklahoma Tourism
1-800-652-6552
www.state.ok.us

Oregon Tourism
1-800-547-7842
www.traveloregon.com

Pennsylvania Travel
1-800-VISIT-PA
www.state.pa.us/visit

Rhode Island Tourism
1-800-556-2484
www.visitrhodeisland.com

South Carolina Tourism
1-800-346-3634
www.travelsc.com

South Dakota Tourism
1-800-S DAKOTA
www.state.sd.us/tourism

Tennessee Tourism
1-800-TENN 200
www.state.tn.us/tourdev

Texas Tourism
1-800-88-88-TEX
www.traveltex.com

Utah Travel Council
1-800-200-1160
www.utah.com

Vermont Travel Division
800-837-6668
www.travelvermont.com

Virginia Tourism
1-800-VISIT-VA
www.virginia.org

Washington, DC Visitors
1-800-422-8644
www.washington.org

Washington State Tourism
1-800-544-1800
www.tourism.wa.gov

West Virginia Tourism
1-800-CALL-WVA
www.state.wv.us/tourism

Wisconsin Tourism
1-800-432-TRIP
www.state.wi.us

Wyoming Tourism
1-800-225-5996
www.state.wy.us/tourism

Canada

Alberta
1-800-661-8888
www.discoveralberta.com

British Columbia
1-800-663-6000
www.gov.bc.ca/tourism

B.C. Ferries
1-250-386-3431
www.bcferries.bc.ca

Manitoba
1-800-665-0040
www.gov.mb.ca/itt/travel

New Brunswick
1-800-561-0123
www.gov.nb.ca/tourism

Newfoundland & Labrador
1-800-563-6353
www.gov.nf.ca

Northwest Territories
1-800-661-0788
www.nwttravel.nt.ca

Nova Scotia
1-800-565-0000
www.gov.ns.ca

Ontario
1-800-ONTARIO
www.gov.on.ca

Prince Edward Island
1-800-463-4734
www.gov.pe.ca

Quebec
1-800-363-7777
www.gouv.qc.ca/anglais

Saskatchewan
1-800-667-7191
www.sasktourism.com

Yukon
1-403-667-5340
www.touryukon.com

Mexico
1-800-44 MEXICO
www.mexico-travel.com

Visit Our Website: www.rvknowhow.com
An informative website offering practical, useful information about RVs, RVers and RVing.

Other Books By Joe and Vicki Kieva

RVing Made Easy
A non-technical book that helps you discover how easy it is to choose, operate, and enjoy your RV.

Extended RV Travel
Answers questions about choosing an RV, preparing for and living on the road for weeks/months at a time.

RVing Tips, Tricks And Techniques
This collection of Joe and Vicki Kieva's popular RV advice columns is a guide for successful RVing.

	Price	Qty	Total
RVing Made Easy	$12.95	_____	$_____
Extended RV Travel	$12.95	_____	$_____
RVing Tips, Tricks	$12.95	_____	$_____
Shipping (USA, $2.00) (Canada $3.50)			$_____
Total (Please send check or money order in US funds)			$_____

Your Name _____

Address _____

City _____ State _____ Zip _____

Mail to: RV Travel Adventures
P.O. Box 5055
Huntington Beach, Ca 92615